TRUE
SWAGGER

GROOMING ESSENTIALS FOR MEN

BO' JONES

MRB Publishing, Atlanta, Georgia
© 2014 Bo' Jones, Atlanta, Georgia

First Printing: 2014

ISBN 978-1-304-87954-7

MRB Publishing
6520 Broad Street
Douglasville, Georgia 30134
www.trueswagger.com

Ordering Information:

Special discounts are available on quantity purchases by corporations, associations, educators, and others. For details, contact the publisher at the above listed address.

U.S. trade bookstores and wholesalers: Please contact

MRB Publishing Tel: (770) 362-2969; or
Email cadmanjones@yahoo.com

Dedicated to My Sons
Graison, Taylor and Paul;

"Do Good...Get Good"

And to my Beautiful Wife,
Christine
Thank you. Without your support and patience, I would
have never achieved my dream.

Love,
Thank You
for your Support!

Bo Jones

CONTENTS

FORWARD

INTRODUCTION

SKIN CARE   9

THE ART OF SHAVING   26

HAIR CARE   35

DETAILS   58

THE SCENT OF A MAN   73

FASHION & STYLE   87

HEALTHY LIVING   134

GROOMING THE MIND   157

TRUE

FORWARD

While there are no hard and fast rules on grooming, it is the personal responsibility and essence of every man to meet head on the challenge of presenting a positive image and style that enhances not only his own personal lifestyle and character, but fortifies the positive images of those surrounding him.

"The Gentleman possessing

True Swagger

is cut from a different cloth".

His fiber is of a higher moral thread count. He demonstrates genuine strength, not just physical in nature, but rather in integrity and persona. He is conscious of his appearance in every aspect of his life, and always seeks ways to *improve* as much. A wise man once said a businessman matches his socks to his pants. A gentleman matches his socks to his mood. It has been said, you should never judge a book by its cover; however a book's cover can be just as important as its content.

In researching for this book, I have drawn on the latest information to present a detailed explanation of the world of grooming for men. While bathroom etiquette is not our number one topic of conversation in the barbershop, after the game or even in the home, we still need to know the basics of what is out there to help make us feel good about our personal appearance and style. Let's face it, many times we find the subject of hygiene and grooming unmanly and embarrassing; but one thing is for sure….when we look good, we feel good. Feeling well about oneself provides a strong foundation for the positive men we are to be.

- Bo' Jones

SWAGGER 1 *A person's style- the ways they look, feel, walk, talk, and dress. How one presents himself to the world. **2** Swagger is shown from how the person handles a situation.*

***3** Swagger is to move with confidence, style and to be calm. **4** Swagger is to conduct oneself in a way that would automatically earn admiration or respect.*

(i.e...."Denzel Washington, Steve Harvey and Barack Obama, George Clooney all have a certain swagger ")

CHAPTER 1

SKIN CARE

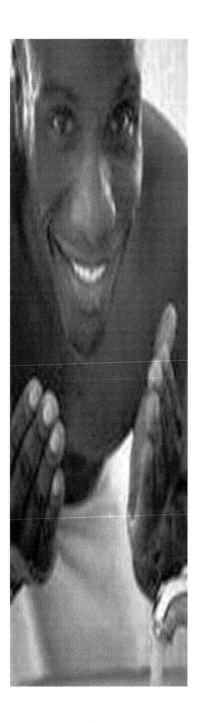

Men and skin care are not exactly the best of friends. Sadly, most of us give more care and attention to our cars, sporting and electronic equipment than we do to our own bodies. While smooth talk and new clothes can give first impressions a lift, we should not remain misled with the view that a few splashes of cologne or after-shave are enough to make any woman fall head over heels, or an employer's mouth water at the chance to give us a job. This is not to say that some of us have not been blessed with great skin and the daily regimen of taking care it... Yet just a little knowledge on how the skin works, as well as how we should take care it can help you to achieve a clearer, healthy tone; free of the razor bumps, spots and blotches that may be dimming your swagger on the brightest of days. Practice the good habits and advice for your skin like Jordan, Kobe or LeBron practiced their jump shots, and you will notice the difference in days.

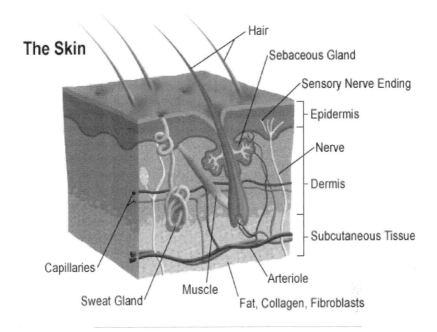

The Skin

Hair
Sebaceous Gland
Sensory Nerve Ending
Epidermis
Nerve
Dermis
Subcutaneous Tissue
Capillaries
Arteriole
Muscle
Sweat Gland
Fat, Collagen, Fibroblasts

SKIN FACTS

➢ All adults have around 300 million skin cells.

➢ The thickest skin on the body is on the palms of your hands and the soles of your feet and can be up to 3/16th of an inch thick (4.7 mm). The thinnest skin is around your lips and eyes and can be less than 1/64th of an inch thick (0.12 mm).

➢ 1 square inch of skin can contain on average 20 hairs, 200 sweat glands, 6.5 feet of blood vessels and 30 sebaceous glands.

➢ Collagen is the elastic property in the skin, that slowly re-duces as you get older, causing the skin to wrinkle and sag as you lose elasticity. The good news is that as men, our skin is slightly thicker than a woman's and contains more collagen; so we are less prone to wrinkles.

TAKE A LOOK IN THE MIRROR

If you look in the mirror before you wash your face, take the time to examine carefully your skin. A man's skin is generally oilier than a woman's because we have larger sebaceous glands, which produce larger amount of oil. This is not a bad thing, for oil acts as a skin protector and can make us less prone to wrinkles. However the down side is that if you have oily skin, you are more likely to suffer from acne, pimples and spots.

As we age the skin goes through a range of changes. During puberty our hormones increase the production of sebum, the skins natural oil. The excess sebum combined with sweat and dirt on the skins surface can clog up our pores. The uninfected clogged pore becomes the blackhead while an infected clogged pore becomes a reddish spot and forms a whitehead. One of these is too many for most of us, and two or more can definitely put a damper on your swagger. You may begin to wonder if they are looking at you or the big pimple on your nose.

What to do...? The use of an anti-spot treatment or cleanser containing salicylic acid or benzoyl peroxide will help clear this up.

During our twenties are more than likely the best time for our skin. As we hit our thirties and forties however, the skin becomes less efficient at removing dead skin cells. This may at times cause the skin to look a little dull.

What to do...? Get a facial. The use of exfoliants and creams to bring your skin back to life is not just for women. If you are unsure what to use and how often to do this, you might check with your barber or an upscale barber-salon. The good ones will be very experienced in providing such services. However, you should still learn and know your own skin type, so you can begin and continue a good plan of caring for it.

OILY SKIN is more likely to suffer from spots and whiteheads than dry skin, and is hard to keep shine-free. If you have oily skin, your pores, especially around your forehead and nose, will be visible and are highly susceptible to blackheads (small, dark pinpricks of sebum). Your face will look shiny most of the time, except when you have just washed it. But wait a minute brother; you do have one major benefit- your skin will age better than dry skin.

What to do...? You should use oil-free products on your face and can probably avoid the use of moisturizers and lotions on the face all together. A mild astringent toner can effective at fighting excessive oiliness. And always keep a clean handkerchief or small towel to wipe your nose and forehead before an important event, interview or taking her on a date.

DRY SKIN is hard to see the pores on dry skin, which need extra care since it is more prone to peeling and flaking. Don't put just any bar of soap into your shower dish -- they're not all the same. Wash with a harsh soap and you'll send your skin's natural moisture barrier straight down the drain.

What to do...? Make sure the surface of your skin is slightly damp when applying moisturizer; this will help seal in the water. Rich creams and cleansers may be more protective than lighter lotions. However do not use products that just sit on the surface of your skin, for no one wants to look at you looking greasy. A night cream (an especially rich moisturizer) may be helpful to enrich your skin while you sleep.

COMBINATION SKIN seems to be a mystery for lots of men. It can be hard to identify and even trickier to treat. Having both oily and dry areas; the T-zone (the middle of the forehead, nose and chin) is greasy with enlarged pores and blackheads, while your cheeks, neck and the rest of the forehead are less oily and lean toward dryness. When it comes to combination skin, the causes are a little bit different for everyone. Men, who had oily skin in adolescence, may develop combination skin as they age. This is because when you are young, the sebaceous gland produce more oils on the skin. A quick way to determine if you have combination skin is to feel if you have greasiness or shininess on the nose or forehead 20 minutes after washing.

What to do...? Avoid putting moisturizers on the oilier parts of your face, but definitely hit those dry areas...they still need hydration. Treat both areas separately in terms of the products you use.

SIMPLY WASH YOUR FACE

Well it sounds easy enough, right? Turn water on, place soap on wet wash cloth and go to work...not so fast gentlemen. True enough

clean skin helps prevent spots and blemishes from forming, but many of us still miss the mark of doing this basic task. Washing with soap and water is not necessarily a bad thing, as long as you thoroughly rinse the soaps off your face. Many relate that tightness you feel after using soap to the skin being clean, but it is actually caused by a temporary pH imbalance between the soap, which is alkaline, and skin, which is slightly acidic. The tightness eases after a few minutes or so.

What to do…? For the best results wash with water that is about the same temperature as the body (98.6° F or 37.0° C). Build up a good lather on your already damp skin. If using a face wash, cleansing cream or gel, be sure to follow the products instruction. Many brands have different versions for different skin types, so use the product that's right for your face.

The term "two-a-days" doesn't just apply to football practice and working out. Wash your face in the morning and at night, especially if you have oily skin. If face washes and soaps leave your face feeling to tight and dry, just use a mild cleanser in the evening when your skin has a build-up of dirt from the day and rinse thoroughly with water, or use a facial scrub in the morning before you shave.

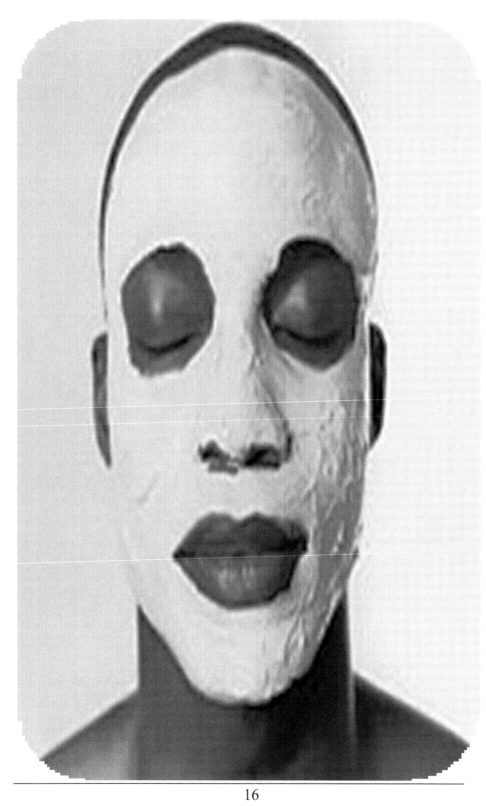

Gender aside, good skin is good skin. Guys, ask a woman, she'll tell you! Having a quality and professional facial treatment done, whether routinely or on a more infrequent basis, will refresh your skin, leaving you feeling and looking younger than you would have thought possible.

So, no matter what you've heard, it's not just for women. Masks do all the things that cleansers, moisturizers, scrubs and toners often need a little help with, such as getting rid of excess dirt and debris. They can also help to tame oiliness, especially in the "T-Zone" (nose to lower forehead) area by absorbing excess oils.

Along with tightening up pores that get clogged with dirt and grime, many facial masks can infuse moisture and oxygen to promote skin renewal. Of special benefit is improved blood circulation, healthier-feeling and looking skin.

If you have oily skin, a mud or gel clarifying mask is a must. The mask will dry to a crust; absorbing debris, oil and dirt from your skin. Do not leave it on more than ten minutes unless otherwise stated. Chose a moisturizing or hydrating mask if your skin is dry or you have spent some time in a dry atmosphere. These should enhance the skin, making it look younger. Avoid your eye area when applying a mask, for the ingredients can aggravate the delicate skin. If you have sensitive skin and are using a mask for the first time, do a test patch to see if you would have a negative reaction.

A good facial mask twice a month might not just make you manlier; its de-stressing effects might make you more able to take on life's challenges. There are upscale full service Gentleman's Barbershops popping up all over the country. These types of establishments usually have highly skilled staff offering full service facial treatments.

THERE IS A FACIAL MASK TO SUIT EVERY SKIN TYPE.
DO YOU NEED ONE? THE ANSWER SIMPLY IS, *YES,* AND SHOULD DO THIS ON A REGULAR BASIS.

Many men will and do have an occasional break-out caused by stress, lack of sleep or perhaps some extra consumption of alcohol on the weekend. The break-out is actually a visible sign of your body telling you to *"slow your roll"*, ease up and give yourself a break.

No matter how satisfying popping them may be, attacking and squeezing them with fingers and nails can break

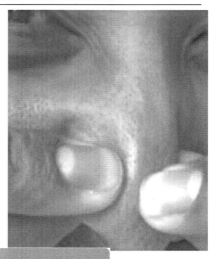

Ok fellas, repeat after me: "No matter how tempting or what my woman says, I will never squeeze or pop my pimples, zits or spots".

the skin and spread infection only to make matters worse. The whiteheads on top of the spot are, in fact, white cells fighting the bacterial infection; they may look bad, but they are actually working in your favor.

What to do…? Well as soon as you notice that spot, get a hold of some benzoyl peroxide; this will help keep the area clean and start to dry it out. If you'd like a more natural solution, try using products that contain tea tree oil, a natural antiseptic, which can also be used on cuts, minor burns or shaving rash. Just using the essential oil itself can work wonders for your skin. A blackhead, or open comedo is a wide opening on the skin with a blackened mass of skin debris covering the opening. Despite their name, some blackheads can be yellowish in color. A comedo is a widened hair follicle which is filled with skin debris (keratin squamae), bacteria and oil (sebum). A closed comedo is a whitehead, while an open comedo is a blackhead. The plural of "comedo" is comedomes".

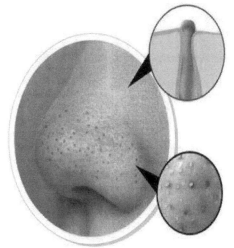

Blackheads are said to be the first stage of acne. They form before bacteria invade the pores of the skin. A blackhead can develop into a pimple, which is also known as a papule or pustule. Blackheads are caused by oil from over active sebaceous glands combined with the dirt and debris of dead skin cells plugging up our pours. This is likely to occur in a high proportion of men during puberty. Spikes in hormone production can result in the high levels of DHT (dihydrotestosterone), a hormone which triggers over activity in the oil glands, resulting in clogged pores. The dirt and oil stretches the pores, making them look larger.

What to do...? Pore Strips (self-adhesive strips designed to lift the blackheads and pull out the debris) can be an effective treatment. While only a temporary measure, if followed by the use of a good cleanser and toner, this can leave the skin clear and less likely to get blemishes. However, remember:

BLACKHEADS ARE CAUSED BY OXIDIZED OIL, NOT DIRT. OVER-CLEANING THE SKIN CAN LEAD TO IRRITATION.

5 TIPS FOR ACHIEVING GREAT SKIN

1. **Drink six to eight glasses of water every day.** Drinking water helps the skin in the process of cell regeneration and renewal. Thirty-five (35%) percent of the body's total water content is in the skin. Staying well hydrated keeps your cells in check, if you are dehydrated (lack of water) your skin will lose flexibility.

2. **Don't Smoke.** Besides the obvious hazardous to your health risk, statistics show smokers develop lower levels of vitamin C, which can increase the signs of aging and wrinkles in the skin. So although you may have an extra glass of O.J. here or there, if you smoke, your body is likely to use the vitamin C up faster than a non-smoker.

3. **Fruit and Vegetables are a must.** Your diet is important not only for your overall health but your skins health as well, and should include fresh fruits and vegetables. Forgo the sweets, the soda and the junk food and focus on taking in food that will improve your body's health.

4. **Get enough sleep.** No matter what else you do, if you are sleep deprived your skin will show it, and certainly the bags under your eyes will be a dead giveaway. Burning the candle at both ends is not the move to maintain true swagger.

5. **Limit your consumption of alcohol.** Drinking takes its toll on your skin and ages you. Drink in moderation not only for your overall health but for the sake of having and maintaining younger looking skin.

True SWAGGER means knowing your limits!

Even if you have oily skin on your face, the rest of your body could well have a tendency to be dry.

What to do...? In addition to your daily regimen of cleaning your body; at least three times a week before your bath or shower, brush your skin with a body brush. You can purchase one from your local Wal-Mart. A soft-haired brush vigorously swept over the body from head to feet upwards toward the heart helps get rid of dry, dead skin (especially around your ankles, knees and elbows), and leaves the skin tingling and smooth. Brisk brushing also can stimulate circulation, which speeds up the elimination of toxins.

To help counteract dryness, a teaspoon or two of olive oil in your bath or during the final phase of your shower can work wonders. If you live in a hard-water area where it's tough to get a good lather with soap, squeeze a shot or two of baby oil in your bath or on your sponge, washcloth used during your shower to help keep your skin soft.

And always follow your bath or shower by applying some body lotion, or olive oil to your still damp skin; particularly to the feet, elbows, knees and hands. It will keep any dry area of skin smooth and help avoid a buildup of dead   skin. This move is an added plus to your swagger...don't believe me....ask her.

The conversation about healthy skin would not be complete if we overlooked the mere fact that in this day and time many men, young and older alike, have chosen to concert their swagger with the display of one if not multiple body piercing's or tattoos.

Whether you regard this a good move or not, the individual statement in both these so called art forms has become increasingly popular. But since this chapter deals with the achieving healthy skin, here are a few facts you do well to consider should you embark on either procedure.

1) With tattooing, microscopic punctures are made in the skin with ink to create a permanent picture, words or symbols. The intensity of the ink will fade over time, particularly if exposed to the sun, but will always remain visible.

2) Removal of tattoos can be costly, painful and lead to permanent scarring. Warning: Never tattoo your girlfriends name on your body. Think about it!

3) Piercing is a puncture wound and some areas like the ears and tongue heal within weeks while the naval, nose and other sensitive areas can take months.

4) In both practices, if the equipment is not sterilized, a nasty infection can result leading to a very painful procedure.

5) Only use a practitioner that has high standards of hygiene, sterilize all equipment, and use single-use tools. This will help prevent the transmission of blood-borne pathogens like hepatitis B, C and HIV/Aids.

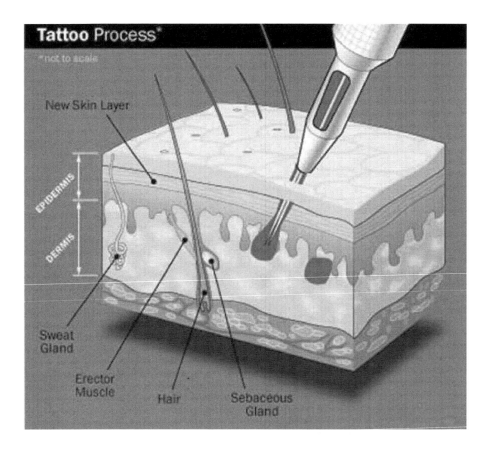

In America, the FDA regulates some of the ingredients in cosmetics worn on the skin, and vitamins, drugs and food additives ingested into the body, but it does not regulate these toxic inks we put under our skin. Their official stance:

"Because of other public health priorities and a previous lack of evidence of safety concerns, FDA has not traditionally regulated tattoo inks or the pigments used in them."

The FDA also does *not* require ingredient disclosure on the inks; they are considered proprietary (trade secrets). Tattoo inks may contain any chemical, including those known to be mutagenic (capable of causing mutations), teratogenic (capable of causing birth defects), and carcinogenic (capable of causing cancer), or involved in other biochemical reactions in the body that might take decades to appear.

Surprisingly, the FDA does not list cancer in their list of potential tattoo risks, citing only infection, removal problems, allergic reactions, granulomas, keloid formation, and MRI complications. The job of testing and legislate the use of tattoo pigments in permanent cosmetics is left to the state.

The price of ignorance...? Although allergic reactions to permanent tattoos are considered rare given the number of tattoos applied yearly (in the neighborhood of 9 million), they can occur. In addition to allergic reactions and the unknown long-term health effects from the metal salts and carrier solutions that make up tattoo inks, there are other health risks involved. Skin infections, psoriasis, dermatitis and other chronic skin conditions, and tumors (both benign and malignant) have all been associated with tattoos.

With the absence of federal regulation to protect you from unqualified tattoo artists, unhygienic tools and application methods, and highly toxic inks, the best advice today is abstinence from tattoos. Although certain tattoo ink ingredients may be plant-based or otherwise considered safe and non-toxic, the truth is that no long-term studies have been performed confirming that they are safe to inject as a permanent cosmetic.

SWAGGER IS NOT THE
PRODUCT OF TATTOOS,
NIETHER ARE TATTOOS THE
PRODUCT OF ONES SWAGGER.

CHAPTER 2

THE ART
OF SHAVING

I ngrained in the true essence of being a man is being able to embellish the coolness and desired smoothness of a clean and crisp shave. Women don't do it, never have and (hopefully) never will. Shaving is one of the most masculine rituals known to man. However, few are the men that have learned to do it well, which is why aside from entrusting our barbers with the task, we avoid the frustration of opening our own personal "nick and bump" factory on our chins, necks and faces each morning.

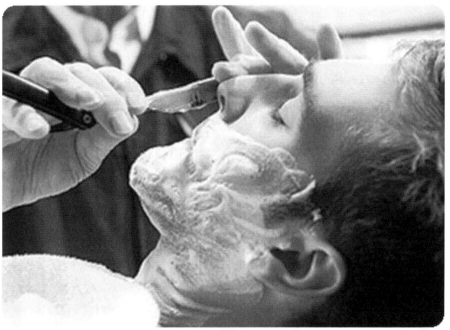

Unless you're growing a full beard, shaving is undoubtedly part of your daily routine. Perhaps you learned to shave as a teenager at your father's side and maybe even still use the same kind of aftershave splash he did. Well, shaving products have come a long way, and for the best shave, you'll need to have more in your bag of tricks than a single-blade razor and a can of foaming shaving cream.

Fortunately, there's no right or wrong way to shave. Whatever works best for your skin and your personal care routine is what's right, but there are some tips and tricks to help make shaving an easier, less irritating experience.

If you're ready for a baby-smooth, bump-free face, the precise technique can help you take the guesswork out of shaving.

But don't grab your six-bladed razor and state-of-the-art shave gel just yet. Keep reading, and you will find out exactly how to prepare your skin properly for a close shave. Removing facial hair with a clean shave, allows us the benefit of taking off that top layer of dead skin cells. Not to mention, done properly, it refreshes your skin, makes you look well groomed and is often a must for work or getting close to your woman. Many ancient African cultures believed a clean shaven face was a sign of youth and virility.

ACHIEVING THE BEST SHAVE EVER

Before you begin to do anything, smooth your fingertips over your face or entire bearded area to feel the direction of growth of your facial hair. You will find that mostly the beard grows downward from the hairline towards the neck, but as you get closer to the *Adam's apple* the hair may actually grow upwards.

Whichever way your beard or facial hair grows, the general rule is that is the direction in which you should always shave. We professionals of the Art of Shaving (Licensed Master Barbers) call this "With the Grain". Your best allies in this task should be; hot water, a clean, sharp razor and plenty of lubrication- be it gels, shaving foam or oil.

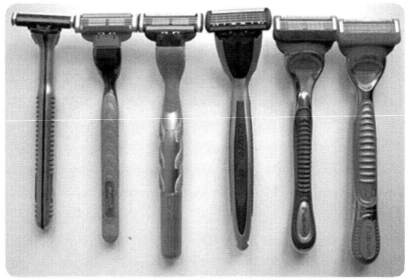

A swivel-headed razor with two, three or even up to five blades will give you the closet shave.

Start by either splashing the face and neckline with several handfuls of almost-too-hot water, or use a face cloth soaked in extra-hot water. Once wrung out, place it over the area to be shaved to soften the hair and the hair shaft for a closer smoother shave.

Gels are the most convenient moisturizer, but foams and shaving soaps are good lubricators also. When you choose a shaving cream or gel, look for a product that's thick and hydrating. The purpose of these gels and creams is to create a protective layer between your skin and the razor, which helps to reduce irritation and razor burn. It creates a slippery surface for your razor blade to glide over, which equals less drag and irritation. Creams and gels also help soften your stubble, and if they don't contain alcohol-based ingredients, they will also help soften and moisturize your skin.

However keep in mind foam contains more air than gels and are therefore less protective against nicks and cuts than a denser gel product. Applying your lubricant with a shaving brush, can help lift the hair or stubble away from the skin, making for an easier shave. If you have the time, don't start shaving right away; give the lubricant a minute to really soften the area to be shaved first. A swivel-headed razor with two, three or even up to five blades will give you the closet shave. It should be replaced every three or four uses, depending on the thickness of your growth (heavier growth will wear out blades quicker). According to Atlanta Georgia based Master Barber, James Pope,

**"USING THE SAME BLADE FOR
DOZENS OF SHAVES IS LIKE
SHAVING WITH BROKEN GLASS;
JUST DON'T DO IT..... DONE
PROPERLY, SHAVING REFRESHES
YOUR SKIN, MAKES YOU LOOK
WELL GROOMED AND IS OFTEN A
MUST FOR WORK OR GETTING
CLOSE TO YOUR WOMAN"**

SEVEN RULES OF SUCCESSFUL SHAVING

1) Do not shave the moment you get up; you will get a closer shave if you wait for at least 20 minutes. This enables the facial muscles to tighten, lifting your stubble away from your face and making it easier to shave.

2) Soften your stubble with a hot, damp towel. Squeeze the towel of excess water and press it over your face for 20 seconds. It feels great and softens any rough areas before shaving.

3) The longer you give your face to warm water the softer your bearded area will be, so try shaving in the shower or bath.

4) Wash your face or use a facial scrub before you shave; apart from cleaning your face, a scrub helps lift the beard from the surface of the skin, enabling the blade to remove it more efficiently.

5) Sounds ole fashioned, but the fact is a shaving brush works best at spreading lather and aids the process of lifting dead skin cells from the surface of your face.

6) When you have finished shaving use a soft, clean towel to gently pat your face dry. Leaving your face slightly damp before applying your shaving balm or moisturizer will help keep your face and neckline hydrated and supple; lessening your chance of getting those undesirable razor bumps.

7) If your beard growth tends to be heavy, you may want to apply a moisturizer to your skin before you apply you lather; this will give an added layer of protection from nicks and cuts.

If you're a man who shaves daily, you'd probably rather watch your favorite sports team lose a championship than walk around with a face and neckline full of these. If you suffer from ingrown hairs, razor bumps; the grand medical term is called *folliculitis*.

Folliculitis is an infection of a hair follicle. It looks like a tiny white pimple at the base of a hair. There may be only one infected follicle or many. Each infected follicle is slightly painful, but the person otherwise does not feel sick. It occurs when the curl of our facial hair is so tight that some hairs do not manage to break through the surface of the skin; instead they grow back underneath 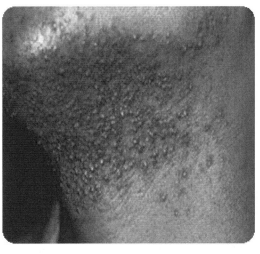 where they are not recognized by the body and are attacked, causing inflammation and infection. Shaving over this area will further aggravate the skin, and the bumps caused by the hairs can easily be accidentally cut when shaving.

Sometimes stiff hairs in the beard area curl and reenter the skin (ingrown hair) after shaving, producing irritation without substantial infection. This type of folliculitis *(pseudofolliculitis barbae)* is particularly common in black men. Each ingrown hair results in a tiny, mildly painful pimple with a barely visible hair curling into the center.

The hair follicles in the beard region are red and inflamed caused by infection with Staphylococcus and aggravated by shaving. This infection brings blood vessels in the area dilate to bring in extra white blood cells to eat the bacteria and other foreign particles gathering at the site of injury.

As a result, dead cells begin to accumulate thus forming papule that turn into pus during the healing process. Any hair in the area gets bound under this formation, cannot exit the skin properly, and worsens the affected area. The hair must be removed to ensure proper and complete healing.

As a Licensed Professional in the Art of Shaving, I often treat this condition, and recommend the following when you shave:

- *Always shave in one direction only. Usually the direction of hair growth.*

- *Do not pull your skin to tight to get a closer shave.*

- *Use a sharp, clean razor with 3-5 edge blades.*

- *Use tweezers to untangle ingrown hairs, and then cut them with your razor or clippers.*

- *Use an aftershave balm that straightens facial hairs. (Bump Patrol or Tend Skin work well)*

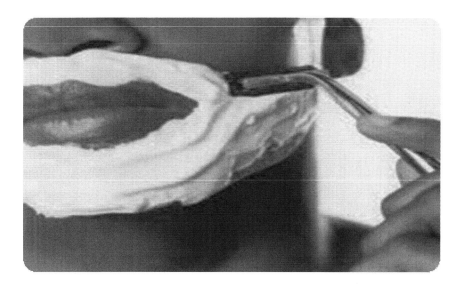

RAZOR BURN is actually a skin irritation. When you shave, you are basically peeling off part of your epidermis, the top layer of skin. The redness is a normal response to tissue injury. Blood flow increases to the area to heal the wound, and blood vessels dilate and become red.

Razor burn is hard to get rid of. Every time you shave again, you re-irritate your skin.

What to do...? Replace your razor. If you're getting a close shave with double-edge razors and disposables, they can really irritate your skin and traumatize hair follicles. The duller they get, the more irritat-ing they become -like a rake dragged over your skin. You may be better off toss-ing a disposable razor and break out a new one after two or three uses. Also, the next time you shave, give irritated skin a break by making sure that it's well-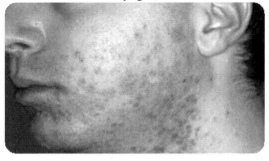hydrated before you graze a razor over it. The best time to shave is after a shower or bath. Your skin won't be dry, and your hairs will soften and stand up, so shaving will be less traumatic.

LATHER, LATHER...LATHERS. WHAT TO USE?

SHAVING BALMS typically combine the moisturizing qualities with an astringent which is a must with shaving. Shaving balms come in many fragrance ranges, which allow you to apply an antiseptic, moistur-izer and pleasant smell all- in- one use.

SHAVING FOAM is a more aerated lubricant (meaning it has more air in it than gel). Always shake the can before applying and make sure your face has been softened and wetted by plenty of hot water. A ten-nis ball size of foam sprayed in the hands should be plenty to do the job. Foam is not as lubricating as gel, but is fine if your beard growth is not heavy.

SHAVING GELS get my number one vote, because of its consistency and lubricating effect. A teaspoon of shaving gel should be enough to remove up to two days growth in most cases. Apply the gel with your fingertips or shaving brush to your warm damp face and watch it turn into a dense cream. If you have time, leave it on for a minutes before starting your shave; this will soften your hairs even more, making them easier to cut.

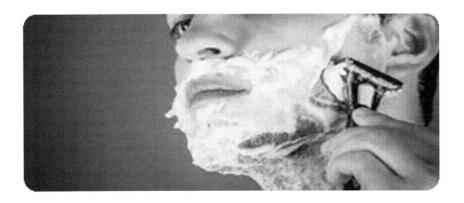

SHAVING OILS can give you the closest shave of all when used correctly. The oil is usually sold in small 20 ml bottles and only a few drops are needed to lubricate an already wet beard. If your razor starts to drag during your shave, continue to splash your face with warm water to reactivate the oil. The small size of the product makes it good for traveling; but the oils can clog your razor quickly. Be sure to rinse and tap away the shaves hair from the blade after every stroke.

CHAPTER 3

HAIR CARE

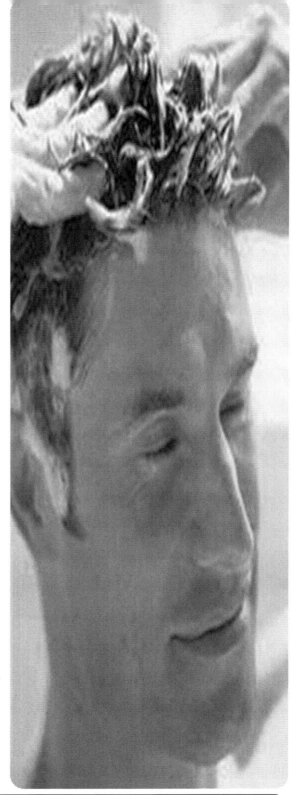

Although it's usually women that sit in beauty salons for hours getting their hair sewn in, teased, curled, dyed, permed, shampooed or flipped; we men sit in a barbershop or attempt to groom our own hair. Yet, while our hairstyles tend to be shorter and may not require as many chemicals to achieve the right appearance, we still employ quite a bit of primping to enhance our SWAGGER when it comes to our head and hair.

CARING FOR MENS HAIRSTYLES

Like your car, computer and body, your hair needs maintenance in order to preserve strength, elasticity, and shine. Because most men's styles are very short, they require regular touch-ups at the barber shop or salon to keep looking their best. In between professional treatments, it is important to use moisturizing products. Be sure to use products formulated for your particular hair texture if available, because very curly hair can become brittle and damaged very easily, increasing the risk of hair loss. With such short styles, you should also consider using shampoo and conditioner with properties to help protect the scalp from dryness and skin damage.

In today's society, there are a variety of men's hair styles to suite anyone's Swagger, but the most popular styles are still, and will probably always be derived from the basic men's cuts which include:

Faded Cuts

The faded haircut is a popular, flattering style that encompasses any type of cut in which the hair is cut short near the neck and gradually gets longer near the top of the head. The hair gradually gets shorter on the back and sides of the head, and it's longest at the top of the head. Any type of gradual transition from short to long is considered a fade. Typically done with clippers, these are easy to manage looks that can be main-

tained in seconds. In order to control the curl within overly curly textured hair, the faded cuts are typically far shorter than for straight hair textures. The edges may be sharply defined or left with a natural definition.

Textured Styles

Short textured hairstyles are very popular today. They are well suited for men who are athletes, work outside, or live an active life-style. This type of cut is very low maintenance, as well. Texturing the hair usually involves a straightedge razor or a pair of thinning scissors. Communicate with your hair stylist or barber about using one of these methods to create dimension in your hair.

A texturized style may require a chemical application which will leave the hair curly or wavy ac-cording to the desired style; or may be textured by razor or point cutting to achieve a desired tex-tured look. If you have a thick or thin head of hair, both can benefit from a short textured hairstyle.

For thick and unruly hair, textur-izing will help to eliminate bulk, allowing your hair to gain shape more easily, rather than being weighed down. The use of a hair gel or lotion will give the hair a soft and moistur-ized look and feel. Getting the best in style out of short hair can be a chal-lenge.

There are, however, many short textured hairstyles for men that can be both easy to manage and appropriate for work or play. If you aren't sure what to do with your hair, but you want to try something new to enhance your Swagger, most professional Barbershops or Salons offer these ser-vices.

This long style, often favored by men with Jamaican or Caribbean backgrounds, consists of thick twists covering the head. The hair may be only as long as the collar or it may extend to the waistline.

Locks, sometimes called dreds are associated most closely with the Rastafarian movement, but people from many ethnic groups have worn locks, including many ancient Hamitic people of North Africa and East Africa ; Semitic people of West Asia; Indo-European people of Europe and South Asia (notably the ancient Spartan warriors of Greece, and the Sadhus of India and Nepal); Turkic people of Anatolia and Central Asia; Some Neanderthals and Cro-Magnon were also known to have worn locks as

described in Paleolithic cave art in Europe, perhaps for spiritual reasons.

When reggae music seemed to have gained popularity and mainstream acceptance in the 1970s, the locks (often called "dreads") became a notable fashion statement; they were worn by prominent authors, actors, athletes, and were even portrayed as part of gang culture. However, locks aren't always worn for religious or cultural reasons.

MEN MAY WEAR THEM JUST FOR "STYLE" WHICH IS PRIMARILY POPULAR AMONG SOME YOUTH TODAY.

Traditionally, it was believed that in order to create locks, an individual had to refrain from brushing, combing or cutting the hair. However, a variety of other methods have been developed to offer greater control over the appearance and shampooing frequency of locks. Together, these alternate techniques are more commonly what are referred to as *"salon"* or *"manicured"* locks.

With the Rasta style in vogue, both the fashion and beauty industries have capitalized on the trend, developing a completely new line of hair care products and services in barbershops and salons alike. Since the rise of the popularity of locks, Black men in the Americas have developed a large variety of ways to wear locked hair.

Afro Styles

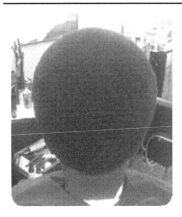

Afro sometimes shortened to 'fro, is a hairstyle worn naturally by people with lengthy kinky hair texture or specifically styled in such a fashion by individuals with naturally curly or straight hair. The hairstyle is created by combing the hair away from the scalp, allowing the hair to extend out from the head in a large, rounded shape, much like a halo, cloud or ball.

Afro is derived from the term "Afro-American". The hairstyle is also referred to by some as the "natural"; particularly the shorter, less elaborate versions of the Afro. In most cases the hair is left untreated by relaxers or straightening chemicals and is instead allowed to express its natural curl or kinkiness. In persons with naturally curly or straight hair, the hairstyle is typically created with the help of creams, gels or other solidifying liquids to hold the hair in place. Particularly popular in the African-American community of the late 1960s, the hairstyle is often shaped and maintained with the assistance of a wide-toothed comb colloquially known as an afro pick. Some afro's are only an inch or two long, while others may be several inches in length for very pronounced styles, such as were popular in the 1970's.

The Afro saw popular resurgences in both the 1990s and 2000s. Today these styles would take varied forms as well as various sizes; from close-cropped natural hairstyles all the way to expansive looks.

Nowadays, more and more men are shaving their heads whether their hairlines are receding or not. Why? Well for starters, men opt for the *"shaved style"* because it looks sharp and intimidating, plus it's practical, easy to maintain, and let's be honest, it knocks another step off one's daily grooming routine.

In addition, the "bare" look is common among A-list celebrities like ***Vin Diesel, Bruce Willis, Michael Jordan, Steve Harvey, and Denzel Washington*** just to name a few. It's trendy, growing in popularity and becoming widely accepted as the norm, even at the office.

Let's face it: One of the main reasons the shaved look is so widely accepted is because it's a logical step for *balding men* to take. Most men have begun to accept themselves as they are. Their confidence and new found Swagger don't need to hide under the dreaded comb-over anymore. And it doesn't hurt that a shaved head allows them to fully showcase their rugged facial features.

Keep in mind, shaving it all off you is far less expensive than having to pay for a conventional haircut every few weeks.

While you will probably save on the cost of shampoo and conditioner, shaves must be redone at least every few days to keep a neat, clean style.

HOW TO SHAVE YOUR HEAD

In order to ensure a smooth shave and prevent "self-inflicted wounds," keep your scalp muscles relaxed and your skin well moisturized throughout the shaving process.

Your best bet is to shave in the shower because the feeling of water massaging your head will help relax your scalp muscles, open your pores and follicles, and soften the hair for a smooth shearing by the razor blade.

LOOSING YOUR HAIR?

Hair loss is something that affects over 40 million men in the U.S. and hundreds of million more worldwide, so clearly it was a bald man who spoke up and said, "I'm not going bald, I'm just taller than my hair". True enough balding men sometimes go through the self-inflicted agony of losing the crown glory society has attached to wisdom and strength.

Feeling blindsided by their traitorous scalp and missing their old hair, some men can get stuck in different stages of the grieving process, unable to move on to acceptance. They start wearing a ball cap or a beanie wherever they go. And they stubbornly stick with the hairstyle they rocked when they were 20, even though it's now making their thinning hair look even worse than it has to. Not knowing how to go bald gracefully, many even resort to remedies that cause even more hair loss.

The main type of hair loss in both men and women is ***androgenetic alopecia***, also known as ***Male-pattern baldness***, which affects around 7.5 million men, usually begins above the temples and can occur at any age; the receding hairline eventually forms a characteristic ***'M' shape***. The hair at the top of the head also thins, progressing to baldness.

Male-pattern baldness is usually inherited and is thought to be caused by hair follicles being oversensitive to dihydrotestosterone, which is produced by the male hormone testosterone. As a result, the follicles shrink and eventually stop functioning.

Other possible causes include physical and emotional stress, as well as medications for depression, acne, and heart disease. There are no cures for male baldness, although medications can slow hair loss. *Minoxidil* lotion, for example, is applied to the scalp and can stimulate regrowth after about 12 weeks. There is also hair transplant surgery, where, under local anesthetic, a small piece of scalp is removed from an area where there is plenty of hair.

Far better to accept the change, but if letting it go all the way has not hit you like a run-a way train yet…then at least keep it as short as possible and decide to fall in love with the shape of your head. Your worth as a man isn't tied up with how much hair you have on your head. If you don't make a big deal out of your hair, no one else will either. After all, *she may just find it quite sexy.* Remember this:

"IT WASN'T YOUR HAIR THAT GAVE YOU SWAGGER TO BEGIN WITH. "

With or without hair, she will love you just the same. Your lack of hair wasn't what made her interested in you from the start; it was your True Swagger, style and personality that she grew to love.

THE GENERAL RULE for BALDING

Keep your hair short. Short hair minimizes the appearance of balding and also gives your hair some lift which makes it look like you have more hair. Some guys don't believe this and try to hold onto to their old styles. But if you've ever seen a guy with a big curly fro and a bald spot at his crown, you've seen how longer hair simply makes bald spots more conspicuous. So go short.

Because hair textures and types are different in all men, there really is no cookbook or cookie cutter remedy to managing healthy hair. However if you follow the basic guidelines for hair maintenance and care, you can easily begin to enhance this part of your Swagger.

Never under any circumstances should you attempt the comb-over. No matter what style you go with, never, ever use a comb-over. And for those of you who once had the long flowing locks of youth, do not fall under the delusion that having a ponytail in the back will compensate for baldness on top. Hair math just doesn't work that way.

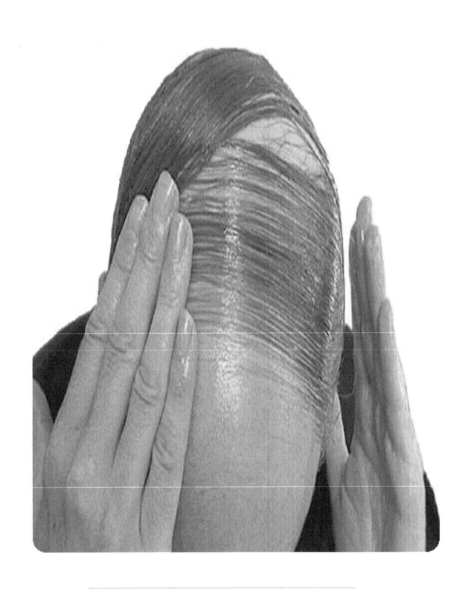

**"NO MATTER WHAT STYLE
YOU GO WITH...
NEVER, EVER
USE A COMB-OVER."**

These days, just about every hairstyle seems to be in fashion at once… long, short, in-between, Beatles-look, locks, Mohawks, ponytails, and military buzz cuts. Some men wear one style at work (parted and combed conservatively to the side) and another (spiked up with styling gel, for instance) when they go out.

The best hair style is one that is suitable for the individual's face shape and hair care preferences. For example, a long, round afro may not be the ideal choice for an individual with a round face, because it will only accentuate that shape. At the same time, someone with a very narrow face may seem disproportionate if they choose a longer style. Furthermore, locks require rigorous care to keep looking their best, while shaved styles, shaved heads, and faded cuts need frequent trims to be stylish.

If you're not sure which way to go, just ask your barber for some advice the next time you're in for a haircut. There's no need to be embarrassed to talk to him about it. Think of your barber like your doctor, hair ...or perhaps in your case, lack of hair is their business. They have seen this stuff a thousand times before.

"WHATEVER HAIR STYLE YOU CHOOSE TO ACCENTUATE YOUR SWAGGER, IT SHOULD ALWAYS BE ONE THAT IS NEAT, CLEAN AND WELL KEPT."

THE BARBERSHOP AND HEALTHY HAIR

Let's face it, even though a good majority of men are making regular trips to the Barbershop for the weekly or semi-monthly shape up or haircut, we just don't tend to engage in conversation with our barbers or other men about caring for our hair and bodies.

I am often amused when I hear of products promoting *"healthy hair"*. There's no such thing as healthy hair. Hair is basically protein and keratin with no blood supply or nervous system and has no reparative qualities. Hair is not alive, so it cannot be healthy. True Hair Care professionals prefer to use the term *"well maintained"* hair.

Once damage has occurred, the only way to repair the hair is to cut off the damaged length. Of course, a healthy looking head of hair starts with clean, conditioned hair followed by a great looking haircut.

But that's just the beginning. Like your car, your hair needs maintenance in order to preserve strength, elasticity, and shine. The following pages discuss my hair care tips for men along with some facts on healthy hair care that we as men really need to know and practice; whether you go to the barbershop or not.

HOW OFTEN DO YOU NEED TO GET A HAIRCUT?

The frequency at which you cut your hair depends on the hairstyle, rate at which your hair grows back, and your budget. It's generally recommended by most Master Barbers to get a haircut every two weeks and a shape-up the week between getting your hair cut. So basically, if it's in your budget, you should be visiting the barbershop every week: haircut, shape-up, haircut, and shape-up. Most men have a specific day they go on each week *(the more routine your visits are, the better).*

SWAGGER TIP: IF YOU'RE MAINTAINING A CERTAIN HAIRSTYLE, LIKE IF YOU'RE TRYING TO PROCESS YOUR WAVES FOR THE FIRST TIME THEN YOU MAY WANT TO WAIT A WEEK BETWEEN WASHES UNTIL YOUR WAVES TO PROCESS.

When changing your style, there's a few things you can do to increase the odds you'll like your new cut. Before you go to the barbershop, try to find a picture of the style you have in mind. A number of magazines are devoted to this topic, and many men's magazines also feature many photographs of different haircuts and styles. Most barbershops and salons also keep these magazines in their waiting rooms. You can discuss your picture with your barber and decide what will look best on you, taking into account the shape of your face and its features, and your complexion.

Pay close attention to how your barber or stylist cuts and styles your new look. Ask about what specific products or techniques that he or she is using. Most barbers and stylists welcome questions and will gladly show you how to get the look at home. Some men may not get a haircut when they are trying to grow their hair long. This is a mistake, as the hair will often end up looking unhealthy. Subtle trims or a quick shape-up will not slow hair growth.

Your relationship with your barber is like any good relationship; communication should be a two-way street. He or she should listen to what you're looking for and give you feedback and advice. A good barber will ask you if you're happy with how your hair looks.. If your barber doesn't communicate at all and doesn't listen to your preferences, it's probably time to pick a new barber.

One of the best parts of the barbershop tradition is that as you par-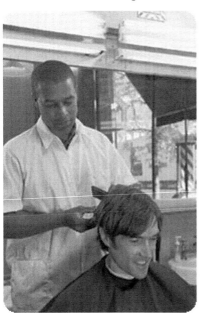take of this manly ritual, the barber can become not only a friend, but someone you're able to count on for good grooming advice and look forward to seeing. After a while, all you'll have to say when you sit down in his chair is "Give me the usual!"

Think back to your last haircut. How did you feel about it when you walked out of the shop? Disappointed? While your disappointing haircut might have been due to poor barbering, it's often the case that your poor communication with the barber was at least partly to blame. ***Barbers can't read minds.*** If you don't tell them exactly what you want, you may get whatever haircut the barber feels comfortable giving. If you want to avoid this fate, you have to learn how to talk to your barber.

USE A GOOD SHAMPOO AND CONDITIONER

The purpose of shampoos in general is to cleanse the hair; relieving it of all dirt and debris. Hair should be lightly moisturized on a daily basis to keep hair from becoming dry and breaking off. Quality Men's Shampoos are a key to great looking hair. They clean follicles and scalps without stripping the good stuff.

Generally you need to shampoo your hair at least *(even if you wear a short style)* every couple of days. A good shampoo and conditioner will help cleanse the hair, add moisture and elasticity, and

> *"Lather, rinse, and repeat" may have been your shower regimen for years, but it's not the best protocol to follow if you want healthy hair. "*

smooth the cuticle to add shine. This is important, so shampooing and then washing the hair with a conditioner is a good routine to acquire.

For example: Shampoo your hair Thursday morning while in the shower then get a haircut or shape-up later that evening. Shampoo your hair with a conditioner Sunday and once again on Tuesday.

Choosing quality products that give your hair texture the desired results should be the goal when selecting moisturizers and finishing products for the hair. **Washing every day with drugstore shampoo?** You're doing your hair more harm than good.

What's wrong with that $3 bottle of supermarket shampoo?

Although economical, it's most likely packed with harsh chemicals known as sulfates, which show up on ingredient labels as "sodium lauryl sulfate," "sodium laureth sulfate," and "sodium lauryl esther sulfate." While these detergents help make products sudsy, they also deprive your hair of its healthy oil, leaving it dry, brittle, and difficult to manage. To avoid these effects, look for a low-sulfate or sulfate-free shampoo, which cleans without removing oil. Sulfate-free shampoos can be difficult to find in drugstores, so ask your barber for a suggestion, or *personalize* your product selection.

Most barbers and stylists recommend shampooing hair only once or twice a week. Why? Because shampooing daily with any shampoo, even with the low-sulfate kind, will strip some oil and dry your hair and scalp. What's more, most styling products like gel and hairspray are water-soluble, so they don't need shampoo to rinse out of hair. Although switching to a once- or twice-weekly shampooing can cause your hair to look greasy at first, it won't after a few weeks, and your hair will be healthier and softer.

Conditioning hair daily helps protect and moisturize it while soothing rough cuticles (the jagged, shingle-like shells that surround hair shafts).

Men with curly hair can benefit the most from daily conditioning, since smoothing the cuticles of kinky hair will help prevent that bed-ragged look, he adds. Just wet your hair in the shower, apply a light amount of conditioner, and rinse.

Not all shampoos, even low-sulfate and sulfate-free kinds, are right for every hair type. If you color over your gray, for example, it's crucial to choose a sulfate-free shampoo formulated specifically for chemically treated hair, since sulfates and other additives can strip tint.

"MOST MEN HAVE BEEN DOING IT BACKWARDS FOR YEARS," SAYS GIBRON "DUKE" SHANNON, MASTER BARBER AT SWAGGER BARBER SHOP IN ATLANTA, GEORGIA. "WE SHOULD BE CONDITIONING EVERY DAY AND USING SHAMPOO TWICE A WEEK INSTEAD OF THE OTHER WAY AROUND...YOU DON'T NEED TO SHAMPOO FIRST TO CONDITION."

Whatever route you take with shampoo, simply apply a small amount to the palm of your hand and rub hands together to distribute the product. Very gently massage the shampoo into the hair and scalp with your fingertips and rinse thoroughly with lukewarm water.

As mentioned, most conditioners can be used every day. For maximum benefit, leave the conditioner on the hair for two minutes (this is a good time to shave your face) and be sure to rinse well with lukewarm water.

TRUE SWAGGERS SHAMPOO PICKS FOR EVERY HAIR TYPE OR NEED

Best for Normal Hair:
Oribe Signature Shampoo, $34;
Paul Mitchell Mitch Double Hitter
2-in-1 Shampoo & Conditioner, $16

Best for Fine Hair:
Aveda Men Pure-Formance Shampoo, $18

Best for Thick Hair:
Pureology Hydrate Shampoo, $25,

Best for Frequent Washers:
Cutler Specialist Cleansing + Conditioner, $22,

Best for Color-Treated Hair:
Phyto Phytocitrus Shampoo, $20;
Oribe Shampoo for Beautiful Color, $37

Best Supermarket Shampoo:
Tigi Bed Head Superstar Sulfate-Free Shampoo, $16

Best for Curly Hair: Aveda Be Curly Shampoo, $21

The condition of your hair is often a reflection of the overall health of your body. Eat well, exercise, drink plenty of water, get enough sleep, and reduce stress in your life. Doing so will result in a healthier scalp and great looking hair. Living well and staying healthy can also increase the rate of hair growth.

Maintain a Healthy Scalp. Hair starts from the scalp, so for hair that's sleek, strong, and shiny, make sure you take good care of your scalp

Use the Right Tools. Don't use a brush on wet hair, when the hair is most vulnerable. When combing through wet hair, use a wide-toothed comb and gently work out any tangles.

Avoid Tight Hats. A tight hat (or ponytail) can cause "traction alopecia," a condition in which hair is pulled out of the scalp. Worn long enough, and the damage can become permanent. A tight hat or ponytail can also cause damage to the cuticle and excessive hair breakage.

Keep it Trimmed. Since the only real way to remove damaged hair is to cut off the damaged section, keeping your hair trimmed regularly will help eliminate split ends. Even if you're growing your hair out, make sure to get it trimmed about every six weeks, but make it clear to your barber or stylist that you only want enough hair removed to eliminate the damage.

Reduce Frizz. Low moisture and protein in the hair can cause frizz. To minimize this problem, use a good moisturizing conditioner. A slick, smoothing serum can be applied to add shine and give the hair a smoother appearance.

COLORING YOUR HAIR

For many guys, going gray is a real blow the self-confidence and to some, gray hair is associated with old age. Conversely, many people consider a full head of gray hair to be quite appealing. Yet many of us have chosen not to gray gracefully and have turned to the bottle for help; the bottle of color that is. Before you decide to color your gray hair, the following are a few things to consider:

1. **A Professional Will Almost Always Produce Better Results.** While there are several "just for men" home coloring kits, a professional colorist will be able to mix exactly the right color formula to ensure a natural looking result. A few companies now produce excellent professional hair coloring for men. I particularly like Bigen, *(a barbershop service often mispronounced Beijing)* that takes about 15 to 20 minutes. The color fades over time, so you don't get a dramatic color change as it grows out.

2. **Regular Coloring Can Be Expensive.** Expect to pay about $30 or $40 (excluding haircut and tip) for men's color treatment and plan on having it done monthly. For professional results, the price is worth it.

3. Color Can Be Hard to Achieve at Home. For any type of color service, I recommend seeking the services of a professional as the results will almost always be more natural. I realize that, for some, this option can be prohibitively expensive. Should you choose to color at home, purchase a product specifically for men, always do a patch test, and follow the manufacturer's instruction.

While many color options are available, as men, we tend to gravitate toward the natural colors of black and dark brown for covering up gray. So if you do feel the need to cover up grey hairs; giving your Swagger a noticeable edge, keep in mind that gray hair can look very distinguished.

The natural process of greying is far less disturbing for men than losing our hair. If grey is not a concern for you, but you are just interested in trying out a new look without the expense of a permanent color, ask your barber about temporary color options to enhance your swagger and appearance.

DANDRUFF

Almost everyone suffers from a dry of flaky scalp occasionally. Your scalp dries, your head itches and small flakes of dead skin fall off: that's the nature of the scalp, it's not a pleasant thing, but it does exist. If you have not had an encounter with dandruff, (also known as ***Seborrhoeic Dermatitis***) which is caused by the ***Pityrosporon Ovule***, consider yourself one of the fortunate 20 percent of the population who hasn't. If you do suffer from this, know that you are not alone and it is easily treatable.

There are many reasons why the skin on the scalp can suddenly shift gears and start shedding profusely. Many people suffer allergic reactions to certain hair products like shampoos, conditioners, etc. These reactions create resistance in the skin to the chemicals in these products. Once this happens, to eliminate what the skin sees as toxic materials, it will increase the renewal rate of producing and discarding skin cells. When the skin cells shed, they carry the chemicals away with them. When the skin perceives that there are no more chemical elements left, the rate of renewal is decreased back to normal levels.

There is a certain fungus, actually a type of yeast, present on the scalp that normally helps get rid of dead skin cells. It's called ***malassezia***, and it ordinarily does not grow out of control. When it does, it is not fully understood why. This fungus growing uncontrollably irritates the scalp, which can result in inflammation and intense skin shedding as the scalp tries to rid itself of the new 'enemy'. Under normal conditions, the fungus works in tandem with the skin to destroy dead, discarded tissue. The fungus may itself by irritated by the allergic reactions some people have to hair care products, as noted above.

There are also psychological factors associated with dandruff. When a person is under great stress, the body 'overclocks' itself to deal with the incredible demands placed upon its physical system. This creates increased bodily cycles, which means that skin all over the body is shed at an increased rate. The cause of dandruff may simply be stress in some people. Stress combined with either of the two causes already mentioned can produce great quantities of skin cells, which could explain dandruff's appearance in some people.

The basic remedy for curing dandruff is the use of an 'anti-dandruff shampoo', which will suppress the yeast activity on the scalp. The active ingredient to look for is Selenium Sulphide. Follow the manufactures instructions, consult your barber and expect the treatment to take a week or two to be effective.

The condition of your hair is often a reflection of the overall health of your body. Eat well, exercise, drink plenty of water, get enough sleep, and reduce stress in your life. Doing so will result in a healthier scalp and great looking hair. Living well and staying healthy will also increase the rate of hair growth.

Since hair is such a big part of your appearance, keeping it well maintained will make you more attractive. So following the simple guidelines mentioned will help you put your True Swagger on another level.

CHAPTER 4

THE DETAILS

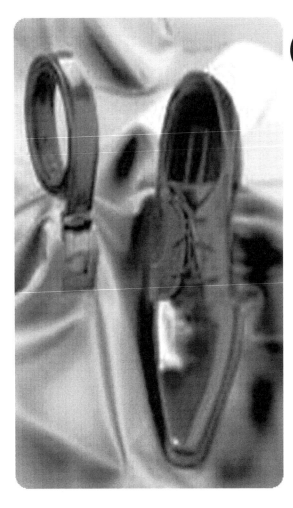

Good Grooming and True Swagger are all about perfecting the fine details of your appearance and persona, so whatever you may do to prove or disapprove peoples first impression of you; it should always start off positive.

Excess hair on your face where there shouldn't be any, ragged fingernails, gnarled feet that look like bear claws, yellow teeth and bad breath will always be held against you. As in dressing well- even if you are simply wearing jeans and a t-shirt, the right pair of foot-wear or a nice watch can make you look stylish; letting your True Swagger rise only if you keep the details in check, you should always look good.

And no matter what

happens to the hair on your head, as you get older, you will become hairier as you age. It won't matter if you think your swaggered up and looking good in your Jordan's, Coogi, Sean Jean, Polo or that Steve Harvey Custom Tailored Suit; if you have dirty nails and hair curling out of your ears and nostrils. If women are embarrassed to be seen with you wearing a pair of sandals, you may as well be wearing a sign around your neck that says:

"I AM A SLOB".

A well-lit mirror and a few simple tools are all you need to improve your chances of being viewed as a well-groomed man. I'm not talking about arching your eyebrows to rival your girlfriends or sisters; *(come on, real men don't do that)* and I definitely don't recommend removing all your nostril hair, but some things need to be kept in check.

Your nose hairs, as well as other hair fibers on your body, create a tough yet flexible barrier. ***Keratin.com*** states that nasal hair protects the

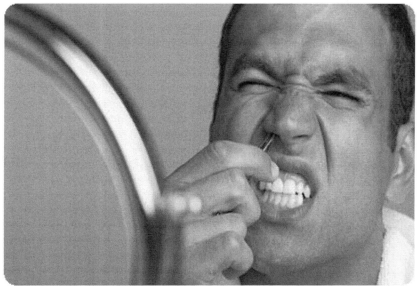

epidermal layer of your skin from small abrasions and sunlight. Nasal hair also has a more specialized function, creating a shield between your body's internal organs and the pollutants of the outside world. When you inhale, you can potentially take in small particles along with oxygen, but nose hairs filter away most debris.

Your best weapon against nasal hair is a pair of fine, blunt-ended scissors (or an electric or battery-operated nasal hair trimmer). Simply push the end of your nose up exposing your nostrils and trim any protruding hairs. Do not go to deep, the hair does help trap debris and pollution when you breathe in. Never pluck these hairs, other than making you cry, the exposed follicles could become infected. The same process can be applied to hair coming out of the ears also. Again, if in doubt on good practice in this, your barber should be able to help you out during your regular visits.

IF YOU HAVE A GRANDPA-LIKE
HAIR COMING OUT OF YOUR
NOSTRILS, SNIP IT WITH
CURVE-TIPPED SCISSORS, WITH
NO SHARP EDGES, OR A
GROOMING DEVICE.

DO NOT PULL THE HAIR.

As your body becomes more mature, your eyebrows may decide to meet in the middle of your brow. While unity can be a good thing in most cases, this is not one of them. There is no big secret to prevent unibrow; either go see your barber or if you are one that just enjoys a little pain, the best weapon is a pair of sturdy tweezers. I don't recommend shaving this area, but if you do, just be aware that the hair is coming back thicker and more prominent every time.

"A MAN'S PASSION IS IN HIS TOUCH..."
- ANONYMOUS WOMAN

If this is true men, we do well to give attention to our hands; apparently she does.

Some of us have a hard time embracing the concept of getting a manicure much less a pedicure for that matter. Something about fingers and toes, when not related to the beauty and elegance of a woman, just rubs our masculinity *(manhood)* the wrong way. But just as going to a nail salon for these services will not make you less of a man, not going wont either; that is if you are willing to employ the *"do it yourself"* method. Either way it needs to be done. A small home manicure set and a desire to be well groomed are all you need to put into practice the following.

HOME MANICURE FOR MEN

1. **Trim your nails with nail clippers, starting from the center of the nail and finishing with a few snips on the sides.**

2. **File the edges smooth with a soft emery board, working in one direction.**

3. **Soak the hands, and then gently push back the cuticles with a cuticle stick.**

4. **Finish by massaging the hands with some rich, moisturizing hand cream or lotion.**

ARE YOUR DAWGS BARKING?

Keeping it real... if it is a struggle to give any attention to your hands, then your feet will suffer all the same. Ragged toenails, hard crusty skin and poor cleaning are the mix for bad, unsightly feet. And although your "Home boys" or Boss may not know what is going on inside those fresh pair of Jordan's, work boots or Gucci Loafers, your girl or mother might be one step away from calling the *EPA (Environmental Protection Agency)* about your feet.

Men are not immune to the same feelings of shame and embarrassment when they deal with toenail fungus, veiny feet or misshapen toes. ***Ugly feet know no limits!*** You will find that being meticulous and consistent with your foot care regimen only helps as time goes on. The more your feet relax the better they look and feel.

They may never be beautiful, but come on men; a little care and attention make the feet feel great, and just might stop her from gagging every time you take off your socks. If you do the basics, she may even be more likely to massage those *dawgs* after a long day. Trust me; a foot massage from the woman in your life is right up there with the other greatest pleasures known to man.

On an average day the feet can absorb about 5 ½ million lbs. of pressure, making them in most cases the hardest-working yet most-neglected parts of the body. The following three essentials used regularly, will make the foundation of your True Swagger feel great all the time.

> A ***Pumice Stone*** (a volcanic rock, lightweight and full of holes); or other abrasive skin removing tool

> A ***Toenail Clipper***.

> A ***Moisturizer or Foot Cream***. (Your foot cream or moisturizer should include a natural odor killing fragrance).

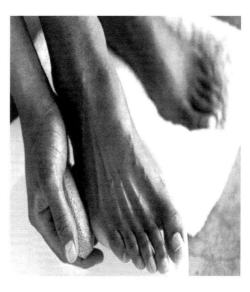

Wash your feet daily. It is not good enough to just let the water flow around your feet; use your hands or a wash cloth to get in between the toes. Good foot care is easy, and an essential part of a man's swagger. The only secret is to keep doing it regularly.

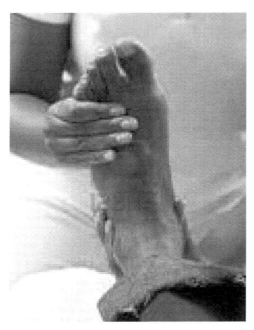

Swagger Tip: Get into the routine of checking your nails and the condition of your feet about once a week. Always groom your hands and feet in private. Unless you are going to the Nail Spa with her, a man tending to his own nails and feet is a big turn-off for women. Be sure to dispose of all trimmings and debris; if she steps on one of your clippings, you stand more of a chance of finding that needle in the hay stack, than getting a foot massage.

1.   After or during your bath or shower, remove any dead skin from the soles and heels by rubbing them gently with a Pumice Stone or metal foot file.

2.   Cut your toenails with a toenail clipper (the larger of the two nail clippers) working from the middle of the nail to the sides leaving a thin white line at the edge of the nail.

3.   Finish by massaging the feet with some rich, moisturizing foot cream or lotion.

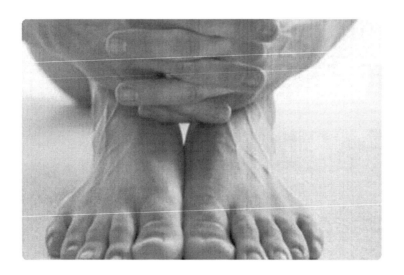

MAKING A COMMITMENT TO DAILY FOOT CARE AND ATTENTION CAN REALLY MAKE A DIFFERENCE IN HOW YOU FEEL ABOUT YOUR FEET.

ORAL SENSATION

Your skin may be looking better than ever; clean, smooth and no blemishes ...but then you opened your mouth and the rich aroma of death took your swagger to an all-time low.

Oral hygiene and good teeth management are as much a health issue as a grooming issue. To have good looking teeth and healthy gums not only make you look younger, but also implies you are looking after your mouth properly. *If your teeth are not clean, people will start to wonder about all of your hygiene habits.* No amount of money, good looks, or wardrobe can fix the damage done to your True Swagger by poor hygiene of the mouth. And to top it off, what woman of any character, class and sense of smell is going to voluntarily put her mouth anywhere near yours without you having a high standard of mouth hygiene?

Good mouth management requires three essential tools:

- **A Toothbrush** (to remove plaque, the bacteria that causes tooth decay and gum disease).

- **Dental Floss** (to remove the debris and bacteria caught in between your teeth).

- A good **Oral rinse** or Mouth Wash.

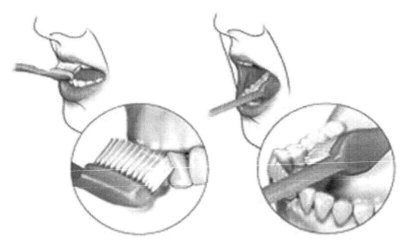

To brush your teeth correctly, clean your teeth twice a day; both morning and night. Take care to reach the teeth at the back of your mouth and making sure you brush the outer and inner surfaces, as well as the biting parts. Spend at least two minutes using a recommended technique, which includes 30 seconds brushing each section of your mouth (upper right, upper left, lower right and lower left. Since most manual toothbrushes don't have built-in two-minute timers, you may want to have a clock handy so you can be sure you're brushing long enough.

Be sure to brush gently along the gum line. Brush your tongue in a back-to-front sweeping motion to remove food particles and help remove odor-causing bacteria to freshen your breath.

While there are several methods of brushing teeth with a manual toothbrush, always ask your dental professional for their recommendation and be sure to follow their instructions.

TYPES OF TOOTHPASTE

These days, you may feel overwhelmed by the types of toothpaste available at your grocery store or pharmacy. Just remember: *The best toothpaste for you is the one you like well enough to use every day.*

Of course, you can buy a few different types for variety or to suit the tastes and needs of your family members. Today, there are toothpastes to meet the oral care needs of virtually everybody, and you can't really go wrong with any toothpaste that has the seal of the *American Dental Association.*

That said, some toothpastes do offer specific benefits in addition to cleaning teeth. Some specialty types of toothpaste include:

Antimicrobial. Antimicrobial toothpastes may contain stannous fluoride, an antibacterial agent that also provides anti-cavity and sensitivity benefits.

Tartar control. Tartar-control toothpastes may contain sodium pyrophosphate which helps to keep tartar from forming on teeth; or better yet, sodium hexametaphosphate, which helps prevent tartar and stain, above the gum line. But if you already have stubborn tartar, tartar control toothpaste won't remove it-you'll need a professional cleaning from your dental hygienist.

Whitening. Whitening toothpastes contain chemical or abrasive ingredients to help remove and/or prevent stains from forming on the teeth. When used regularly, whitening toothpastes can reduce the appearance of stains and make your teeth look whiter.

FLOSSING

Simply put…

"Floss the teeth you want to keep".

Dental Floss is not just for visits to the dentist; we should all be doing it, at least at the end of each day. Otherwise that speck of fried chicken from Big Mamma's last week, which brushing alone will not remove, will quietly breed a host of tooth-boring bacteria and may cause gum infection as well as a cavity.

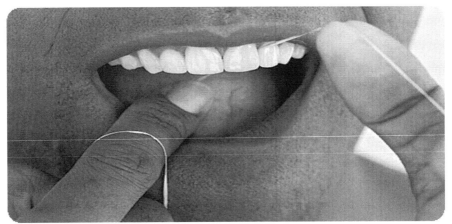

To remove bacteria from between your teeth, use a 1-foot strand of floss; wrap the ends around your index fingers leaving about 4 inches to work with. Start with the floss against the gum between a pair of teeth and gently draw it straight out away from the gum, taking any food and debris with it; repeat if necessary. Be careful not to bring the floss down too hard on your gums, as it can make them bleed.

MAKE FLOSSING YOUR TEETH A REGULAR, DAILY PART OF YOUR DENTAL CARE ROUTINE, AND YOU MAY BE MORE LIKELY TO KEEP YOUR TEETH AND LESS LIKELY TO NEED DENTURES LATER IN LIFE.

THE SWAGGER KILLER

Just as important as the state of your teeth, is suffering a blow from what one might call the **"Swagger Killer"**. Because no matter how smooth your persona, good looks and style are, bad breath can kill your swagger in one whiff. This should not be a surprise if your diet consists of beer, garlic bread and onions. Yet even the smell of these foods can be overcome.

Bad breath is caused by bacteria at the back of the tongue and sides of the mouth, which the tooth brush is some-times unable to reach. However, it will help if you gently rub your brush over your tongue when you clean your teeth. Regularly scraping with an inverted spoon or

tongue scraper is also a good idea. Often times you may not know you have bad breath unless an honest friend tells you.

While breath mints, minted gums and mouthwash are helpful, there effect is often temporary; only masking the bad smell with another smell. It is still far better to formulate the habits of brushing twice a

day, flossing regularly and scraping your tongue of bacteria. If the problem persists see your dentist.

We all want a smile that people notice, but a charming smile doesn't come easily. It requires some extra work to help keep your teeth and gums handsome and healthy. Here are a few tips to help you keep your mouth healthy for years to come.

6 TIPS FOR HEALTHY TEETH AND GUMS

1. **See the dentist.** Many men don't go to a dentist until they feel pain, but if they had gone to a dentist earlier, that pain may have been prevented. A dentist can check for potential problems and treat them before they're serious.

2. **Be gentle.** While brushing as hard as you can may remove more dirt, it will also cause damage to your teeth enamel and your sensitive gums. Brushing too hard really just does more harm than help. Brushing your teeth gently with your toothbrush at a 45 degree angle gets rid of most of the germs and plaque without ruining your teeth.

3. **Brush longer.** The average person brushes their teeth for about 45 seconds. To properly clean all surfaces of your teeth, you need to brush for a full two minutes. Make sure you're getting to all the hard to reach places and not just brushing the easy places over and over. And remember to brush at least two times a day.

4. **Stay soft.** Just as you shouldn't brush too hard, you shouldn't use a toothbrush that is too harsh for your teeth. All toothbrushes have "hardness factors"; you should choose a toothbrush that is soft or extra-soft. Avoid brushes that are rated medium or hard; they'll damage a good-looking smile.

5. **Don't stop with brushing.** There are vast expanses in your mouth that can't be cleaned using a toothbrush. All those cracks and crevices between your teeth need cleaning too. That's why you should floss and use mouthwash every day. They get in all those hard to reach spots where bacteria love to hide.

6. **Watch what you eat.** In addition to properly cleaning and caring for your teeth, you can keep your smile tight by keeping the rest of your body healthy with a proper diet. You should get adequate amounts of calcium, phosphorous and Vitamin D to help keep your teeth strong and charming. Don't forget to get enough Vitamin A and C for good gum health.

THE ESSENTIAL GROOMING ROUTINE FOR MEN

As a recap on the essential principals for good hygiene, the following is a sample routine that is a basic ***must*** in improving your **True Swagger**.

Daily:
Brush teeth, floss, rinse with mouthwash
Shower or Bathe & Moisturize Body and Face
lightly moisturize hair
Brush/Comb/Style Hair (including facial hair)
Apply Deodorant
2-3 dabs of cologne

Nightly:
Moisturize feet
Brush any dirt from underneath nails

Thursday
Shampoo & Condition Hair

Friday or Saturday:
Hair cut or shape-up

Sunday:
Cut nails
ManScape (trim excessive body hair if desired)
exfoliate face and body

The Grooming Routine is all about discipline and efficiency. Having a set routine saves you time, sharpens your organization skills, and most of all takes your Swagger to the next level.

Lastly, grooming goes beyond the products used but extends into having a healthy diet and exercise routine. Having at a minimum a quickie calisthenics workout each morning and/or at night will go a long way. To maintain healthy skin, hair, and nails eat foods or take vitamin supplements with Vitamin E. Most importantly drink lots and lots of water. We will talk more about this in Chapter 7.

CHAPTER 5

THE SCENT
OF A MAN

The Fragrance you wear sends a personal message to the world about how you see yourself and how you want to be seen; so it's worth investigating and familiarizing yourself with the various types and families of "smell good" on the market. You may be simply wearing a pair of jeans and a t-shirt, but with a splash of the right and refined "smell good"… and you'll have every woman on the planet hearing verses of Jill Scott's *"He Loves Me (Lyzel in E Flat)"* in her head as you pass by. However, having the wrong scent on with that Steve Harvey pin-stripe suite and you may be confused with **Pepé Le Pew** (the Warner Brothers cartoon Skunk with a malodorous scent).

BUYING "SMELL GOOD"

The general routine for buying "smell good" or fragrance is; see nice bottle, open nice bottle, smell fragrance…, if it meets the pitch of our nose and wallet we buy, if it doesn't, it's on to the next one. Trial and error seems to be the method of choice for most.

Your choice of cologne can be as make-or-break to your personal style and Swagger as much as your choice of shoes. It goes without say, but we will state it; the same aroma can smell different depending on who is wearing it, so test any potential fragrance on your *own* skin before buying it. The wrist is the ideal place. Many salespeople will spray samples on a card, but this will still not tell you how the fragrance will smell on you.

In general, well-made cologne can costs between $75 and $200. Less expensive fragrances have usually been made to be sold in mass quantities and are less complex to make. On the flip side, a scent that's more expensive than $200 is rarely worth it. Even the priciest ingredients, such as vetiver, iris, and jasmine, shouldn't cost more than that to bottle.

Men are generally not at ease going to the store and buying cologne. Aside from just letting your wife or mother tell you what smells good, here's a step-by-step guide to avoiding buyer's remorse and maybe even finding yourself a signature scent to help set your Swagger apart from the rest.

LEARN THE SCENTS

There are four categories of men's fragrance:

COLOGNE is the strongest fragrance a man can by, but should not be confused with woman's perfume, which is an even more concentrated form of scent. Cologne should be used sparingly because of its strength and, although it is expensive, generally is the most economical because a little can last up to six hours.

EAU DE COLOGNE or EAU DE TOILET is a weaker form of cologne, which can be splashed or sprayed more liberally on the body- and the scent will last approximately four hours.

AFTERSHAVE is the weakest aroma, and can pack quite a stinging punch since it has the highest alcohol content. The alcohol acts as an astringent on your bearded area and as an antiseptic to protect clean shaven skin. However, alcohol is very drying, so you may want to use an aftershave *lotion* if you have naturally dry skin.

ESSENTIAL OILS are highly concentrated extracts of flowers, plants and herbs, which, apart from smelling good, can be used to enhance your mood, alleviate stress, cure headaches and aid digestion. Here are five essentials you may want to keep in the medicine cabinet or around the home *(these oils are highly concentrated, so only one or two drops are really all you need to use at a time)*.

Lavender is good for relaxation and sleep (a few drops on the pillow or in your bath can help depression and in a cold compress can ease swelling.

Peppermint is a decongestant that will clear nasal passages. Add a couple of drops to a bowl of hot water place a towel over your head and inhale the vapors for relief and cure of headaches.

Tea Tree is powerful antiviral, antibacterial oil that can be used directly on the skin to clear up spots, rashes and helps cure warts, herpes and athletes foot.

Eucalyptus is antiseptic, so added to bath water when you have a cold or flu will help relieve a sore throat, congestion and sinusitis.

Rosemary stimulates both the memory and mental faculties. A few drops in the bath or steam room after a workout will relax strained muscles.

Classic fragrance has three layers of scent, called *Notes*; top, middle and base. The ***top note*** is what we smell first right after applying it and usually only last about 15 minutes before fading. Then a progression to the ***middle note*** occurs, the main core of the scent. That's right,

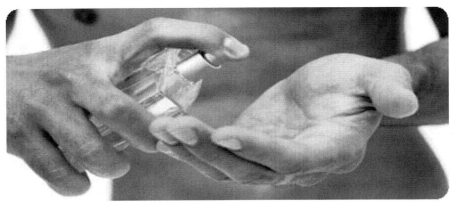

it takes about 15 minutes for a fragrance to truly seep in and mesh with our body chemistry. Now that you have reached the heart of the aroma, this is the point at which you should really decide if the fragrance truly suits you and your ***True Swagger*** or not. The middle note then becomes the ***base note*** after you have been wearing the fragrance for a while and is truly mingled with your natural scent. The base or bottom note is the final signature of fragrance that can linger for hours after applying the product. As it continues to blend with your own body, heat and sweat will emphasize the aroma; ***so never wear cologne when you are going to workout.***

CLASSICS ARE ALWAYS GOOD

Men's cologne classics have made a huge comeback, revived initially by the new Italian fashion designers, who like them for their complexity and rich combination of scents. The great thing about the classics is their reliability; you know what you are getting. They also date from a period when men's fragrances were more discreet, so they lack the orchid and aromatic wood- heavy notes of today's best-selling colognes. This means that if you are unsure about colognes, you can start with a classic fragrance; it is unlikely to be too extreme a smell.

There are of course many fragrances to choose from. Half the fun with men's fragrances is finding the good ones. The other half is of course wearing them.

SWAGGER TIP: WOMEN HAVE A STRONGER SENSE OF SMELL THAN WE DO, SO TAKE ONE WITH YOU WHEN YOU SHOP.

FRAGRANCE FAMILIES

The four bands of fragrance families on the following chart indicate broadly the individual characteristics of some of the top men's scents, describing them as *oriental, woody, spicy or citrus*. But in addition to being categorized into one of the fragrance families, there is also more specific and detailed information that you can only gain by trying out the scent on your own body and seeing how it mixes with your natural body chemistry.

Acqua di' Gio' pour Homme by Giorgio Armani, for instance belongs to the citrus family. In addition to its fruity characteristics, which give it freshness, it also has a marine note, making it smell sporty and summery. A world away from the Armani scent is Gucci Envy for Men, which is a woody fragrance that also has amber and oriental notes.

When you are trying out a new scent, the two most important deciding factors are: do you like the smell on your own skin; immediately after applying it and a while later, and does anyone gag when you walk by. Get those two things right, and your smell cannot fail to enhance your True Swagger and image. And I don't know of a woman who doesn't like a man who smells good.

Oriental
Warm, sensual, seductive, mysterious
JOOP! Homme, JOOP!
Obsession for Men, Calvin Klein
LeMale, Jean Paul Gaultier

Woody
Warm, elegant, precious, mysterious
Polo, Ralph Lauren
Gucci Envy for Men, Gucci
Fahrenheit, Christian Dior
Heritage, Issey Miyake

Spicy
Fiery, exotic, rugged, expressive
Bleu, Chanel
Armani Eau Pour Homme Giorgio Armani
Canali Men,
Carolina Herrera 212 Men

Citrus
Vital, fresh, natural, invigorating
Acqua di Gio pour Homme, Giorgio Armani
Eau Sauvage, Christian Dior
Adolfo Dominguez – Black
Burberry Men

WHAT *SHE* WANT YOU TO HAVE

Most men wear cologne for the simple reason that they want to be more attractive to women. For men that have been searching for that great cologne to attract women, here are some of the top choices according to women that were polled. This should help you through your search for your scent of the season.

Acqua Di Gio by Giorgio Armani

Acqua Di Gio is a sent created by Giorgio Armani Company. According to many women this cologne offers a dark scent that is kind of heavy and a bit old fashioned. However, they do not feel that this is a scent to be used by old men. Acqua Di Gio is recommended for wear during the evening hours. A 3.4 ounce bottle of the scent sells for around **$75**.

PHILOSOPHY Amen Spray Cologne

Amen is cologne by **Philosophy**. According to women this is a scent that simply draws you in. Women want to get closer to you so they can smell it better. Amen is an alluring, nice scent that has sex appeal. This is a great choice for men that want a scent that is not overpowering, but rather subtle. A 2 ounce bottle of Amen by Philosophy runs about **$42**.

The Big Pony Collection # 1 by Ralph Lauren

Big Pony is a scent from **Ralph Lauren**. Women are drawn to its scent because it smells expensive. It is a rich scent that is full of flavor. As with most things associated with Ralph Lauren, many women feel like this cologne is for the all American male. Big Pony by Ralph Lauren currently sells for around **$67.50** for a 4.2 ounce bottle.

Giorgio Armani Code Sport

Sport Code by Armani offers a really intense fragrance. This is a sporty scent that reminds many women of muscular men that are heading to the beach. This is the perfect choice for the spring and summer months as it is fresh and sporty. The cologne by Armani is one of the most popular men's colognes for a reason. It sells for around **$45.50** for a 2.5 ounce bottle.

Giorgio Armani Code Ultimate

Another favorite for women provided by **Armani is Code Ulti-mate**. The scent is simply described as romantic. Women feel that men that wear this cologne really care about how they look and smell. Code Ultimate currently sells for around **$85** for a 2.5 ounce bottle.

"IT HAS BEEN DETERMINED THAT MOST WOMEN ARE MORE ATTRACTED TO A MAN BECAUSE OF THE WAY THEY SMELL AS OPPOSED TO THE WAY THAT THEY LOOK. THE REASON FOR THIS IS BECAUSE ACCORDING TO SCIENCE ATTRACTION HAS A LOT TO DO WITH THE SENSE OF SMELL. WHILE IT IS NOT VERY NOTICEABLE, IT IS ONE OF THE FIRST THINGS THAT A PERSON WILL NOTICE ABOUT A MEMBER OF THE OPPOSITE SEX. THIS IS ONE OF THE MAIN REASONS THAT THE MEN'S COLOGNE BUSINESS IS SO SUCCESSFUL."

For many men, finding the right cologne fragrance to match their indelible spirit can be quite the undertaking. Though it might seem at first like an impossible task to test each and every brand and model, especially when that requires several trips to a department stores fragrance counter; take solace in the fact that there are plenty of other men in the same boat.

The fact is; there is no single best cologne for men. Every man is different, and every nose is different too. The trick to finding the best men's cologne for you is to figure out *what it is that you want your scent to say about you.*

In order to capture this male nature, many of the top brands of men's colognes have come up with sensual scents for men to wear.

These colognes are a *must* for men who want to feel seductive, sensual, and sexy for their woman. While they are not cheap, they are some of the top luxury, sensual and sexy colognes available that every man should give a try.

Acqua Di Parma Essenza Eau de Cologne

This luxurious scent is offered at a price of **$150** for a six ounce bottle. The scent is offered by the design house of Acqua di Parma. Acqua di Parma has been around since 1916 and throughout the years the company has perfected their scents for both men and women. Colonia Essenza offers a blend of lavender, citrus, and rosemary. The scent is recommended for wear in casual situations. Of course, this is a great scent for any type of situation that you find yourself in as it offers a wonderful blend of fresh smells.

GRABAZZI by Gendarme

Grabazzi for men is offered by Gendarme and is top cologne for men for many reasons. A 10 ounce bottle sells for around **$120**. *This is cologne for the man who is passionate about everything.* It offers a deep musky and warm scent that is mixed with spicy carnation and cola berry. The fragrance was created by Topper who says that the scent guarantees that you will be a product of success when you spray it on.

Of course, this is the creator talking, but he does have a point, you will have to swat the women off of you when you are wearing this great cologne.

Amouage

Dia Cologne is offered by **Amouage** and sells for **$179** for a 1.7 ounce bottle. This luxurious scent for men is perfect for wear every day as well as for those special occasions. It is both vibrant and sophisticated. The notes of the cologne include Pallisander, amber, patchouli, leather, vetiver, plum blossom, orris, Ylang Ylang, peony, labdanum, frankincense, cardamom, bigarade, and cistus. *This cologne has a five star rating and is perfect for every man.* You will want to make sure that you keep this scent on constantly.

Creed Millesime Imperiale

A 2.5 ounce bottle of Creed Millesime Imperiale is sold for around **$155**. This great men's cologne is a timeless scent that is recommended for daytime and casual wear. It is appropriate for wear throughout the year as it offers a tropical scent for warmer weather and has enough heart to get you through the winter. This is my personal favorite by far.

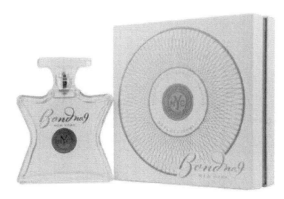

Bond No. 9 West Broadway

West Broadway by Bond No. 9 offers a great scent that is full of surprises. The scent offers notes of flowers blended with cracking grass and green lemon. These scents combine with a pure musk for a scent that is simply tantalizing. The price for a bottle of this great cologne is around **$235**.

KEEP IT SIMPLE

If you use a fragranced soap when you wash in the morning, followed by a deodorant and then splash on cologne, you will be a walking cocktail of aromas. If you want to wear cologne, it is far better to use fragrance-free products on your body, or at least products from the same range.

Apply fragrance only after washing yourself. *Never* use cologne to cover up another bad odor; it doesn't work and you will end up smelling of a sickly combination of body odor and musky sandalwood or worse. In the "smell good" game, less is definitely more. A few minutes after you apply it the scent may leave your nose, but trust me, it's still there. You want your fragrance to be smooth and pleasant, not offensive or invade the space of others.

WHERE TO PUT IT

Simply stick to the familiar territory, such as behind your ears, your neck and upper chest. Keep a bottle of fragrance with you if you go out right after work; a quick wash up and refreshing splash is a good idea before hitting the night.

KEEP IT COOL

If you do spend top dollar for a nice scent, keep it in a cool, dark place, *(not the refrigerator)* where it will last longer and stay fresher. Never leave a bottle of cologne in direct sunlight, which will ruin its smell and color. Air will also affect the fragrance and color, so always replace the top after use.

CHAPTER 6

FASHION SENSE

For many, style is much deeper than articles of clothing; it's a statement of identity. Dressing well is not about buying the latest pair of Jordan's, Italian leather shoes, designer jeans or a tailored made suit; wearing it with some "bling" and imagining everyone is thinking, "Wow, LOOK AT THAT GUY". Rather, you should be dressing to fit the shape of your body and the kind of world you have to live, work and function in. So if you have to wear a suit to work, it shouldn't feel boring and conventional.

You should be enjoying the benefits of the *process* of getting dressed every morning; knowing that the color, weight of the cloth and the cut of the suit will play a major role in how it looks on you. If your work environment allows you to be more casual, getting dressed can still be a minefield: should you wear slacks and a polo, jeans or khakis, collared shirt or t-shirt? And the most danger is when we try to get a handle on what to wear in the evening, at a weekend function, on a date, interview, in a court of law(well, you never know); this is where most of us slip up or at least start to question our own fashion senses.

In the world in which we live, women's fashion tends to go from one end of the spectrum to the other at a pace only they can predict. Howeve, Menswear evolves and moves at a much slower pace, giving certain styles greater longevity and classic appeal.

So, as a man, ***there is little excuse for not dressing well***. All it requires is simply a little thought to work out what you need to wear for what occasion. Then follow a few basic rules about what goes with what, and how to recognize the best styles for your body type and shape.

"THERE IS LITTLE TO NO EXCUSE FOR TODAY'S MAN NOT TO DRESS WELL...WE ARE THE ORIGINATORS OF TRUE SWAGGER"

There are only two basic categories…those who wear boxers and those who wear briefs. You rarely hear of a man wearing both at the same time. And there is a reason they are called underwear *(despite the bewildered look of sagging many have confused with Swagger)*; the garment is meant to be worn *completely* under the pants. Whatever your preference, for sports activities supportive Lycra and cotton mixed briefs hold things in place better than loose boxer shorts. And for the well-dressed man, avoid novelty underwear at all times; you never know when you may have to remove your pants, and those boxes with the 'lips all over them' or your favorite childhood cartoon character may not be a good look.

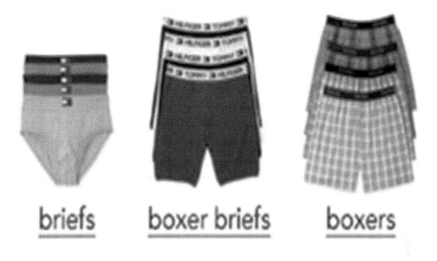

briefs   boxer briefs   boxers

It may seem kind of ridiculous to judge how fashionable underwear is, especially since only a minority of people actually sees this article of clothing. These days though, a man will spend time on such detail, especially when he has an important date or when he feels that an extracurricular activity is going to take place.

According to The True Swagger Underwear survey, 58% of men prefer briefs, 17% prefer tight boxers, and 25% prefer roomy boxers. This survey clearly indicates that a large majority of men don't follow fashion trends and prefer to stick to what they know. A whopping 89 percent of women prefer boxers over briefs; food for thought fellas.

If you're tucking your shirt into your pants, then you should wear a belt; even if it's casual Friday at the office. I recommend you wear a belt at all times, although it's not mandatory on certain casual occasions.

Simple rules for wearing the right belt:

- Wear the same color belt as your shoes.

- Avoid big buckles that draw attention to your waistline (especially if you have a few extra pounds in this area).

- Lighter colored and fabric belts should only be worn with casual clothes.

- When you wear a dark suit your belt should be darker than the suit fabric (which usually means black).

- If you can afford it, don't sacrifice quality, go for the best full grain leather or a cheaper belt that has been treated to make it look grainy.

It's also important that your belt buckle matches the other accessories in your ensemble, so wear a silver belt buckle with accessories in the same color "family," like platinum, stainless steel or white gold.

For men wearing jeans, a wider belt should be worn, if you opt to wear a belt at all. The belt can either be leather (regular leather, suede, nubuck, or pebble grain; all of which look great with denim, tweed and wool), or cotton (canvas included). As well, watch out for the buckle; opt for a heftier buckle when wearing jeans. And never wear a thin belt with your jeans; leave that to the ladies.

As relaxed and casual today's men's fashions might be, formal style holds a sacred and untouchable place in the industry. No matter how much things change, you will always need one form or another of formalwear. The fact that formal attire has changed little in the last half century should be testament enough about its longevity, consistency and importance to a man's style.

Now most of us have to ball on a budget; so, if you are dressing on a budget, one of the best pieces of advice is to just buy off-the-rack suits with the best fit possible, then take yourself to a tailor for some custom adjustments. Small alterations are not that expensive.

Though you may not have the funds to go out and spend a ton of money on your suits, keep this one thing in mind; why spend money at all on a suit, if you are going to look like a hobo in it? Spend just a little more to get it to fit properly!

THE SUIT, IN SHORT, IS ONE OF THOSE THINGS THAT NO MODERN, STYLE-CONSCIOUS MAN SHOULD FIND HIS CLOSET WITHOUT.

Suits are like neck ties: if you're going to own just one, start with the most basic style. In the case of the suit, that means one in **black or gray** fabric. These two are the traditional colors of men's suiting, and therefore the most formal. Although you can use them for casual events too, they'll generally satisfy the dress code in most formal of settings.

Today's style conscious man is fortunate because you have a very wide selection, with options being available for everything from cut to color and shade. For the latter, men's fashion makes use of a very simple rule of thumb:

THE DARKER THE COLOR OF YOUR SUIT (OR ANY ARTICLE OF CLOTHING FOR THAT MATTER), THE MORE FORMAL IT IS.

Because this should be the most formal, and thus the most impressive item in your wardrobe, getting a suit tailored is worth the sometimes costly process. A tailored dark suit will more than effectively satisfy and enhance your True Swagger.

ONE LIGHT SUIT

Men from temperate climates don't always prioritize it, but a light suit is at its strongest when the weather is at its warmest. Typically made of unlined cotton, lighter wools or linens, a suit in tan or khaki gives you the level of sophistication that a suit provides, but adds a dose of levity that's appropriate for summer and tropical heat.

Navy is often regarded as one of those in-between colors in men's fashion; you can wear it with your best necktie and dress shoes, but you can also throw it on with a casual tee. It's no different in the suiting department. Navy serves as the color that's more casual than black or gray, but still manages to dress up your outfit considerably.

Here's where you can get away with a suit that's bought from the store. Because the navy suit is less casual and therefore less demanding than its more formal brothers, you don't have to pay as much attention to razor sharp cut and fit. Of course, having a suit that fits you better than usual would still be a strategic investment, even in navy.

The cool thing about the navy suit is that it's very easy to use the components as separates. The jacket can be thrown on over a shirt, jeans and necktie when you want to go for dressy casual, while the pants can be paired with polo or a tee for a high-low look.

RESPECT YOUR BODY TYPE...
OR CHANGE IT!

Mr. Slim has long limbs and should counteract his vertical height by wearing cloths and colors that can give him an appearance of bulk. Lighter colors and more full-breasted styles are for you. Plaid patterns and window-checks (large squares) can imply bulk. The Slim built man should avoid vertical lines, such as pinstripes, which only emphasize their narrowness.

The Average Joe with a normal or regular body shape, which is neither lean or stocky and off proportionate build, is the most versatile to clothe. You can get away with ***almost*** any style. Choose more fashionable cuts of suit, cut to the body. Single-breasted suites of three or four buttons are the more stylish suits today. Choose a higher buttoning style if you are self-conscious about your middle, as it draws the eyes to the chest rather than your belly.

Mr. "Stocky" is characterized by a thick neck; short limbs and a square, sturdy torso (think Cedric the Entertainer, Bruce Bruce, Ruben Studdard). With this body shape you will want to create the illusion of tallness to counteract the squareness of your body. Vertical lines, such as pinstripes, and a high buttoned jacket (of at least three or four buttons) finishing just below the chest. Avoid large cuffs at the bottom of your suit, which shortens the leg. And avoid checks or plaids, which emphasize width.

TRUE SWAGGER STYLE GUIDE TO FIT

JUST RIGHT   **TO SMALL**   **TO BIG**

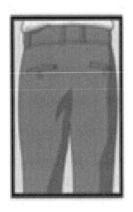 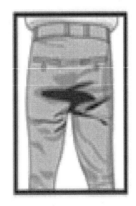 

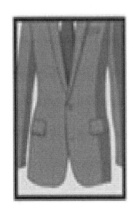  

GOOD FIT   **TO SHORT**   **TO LONG**

 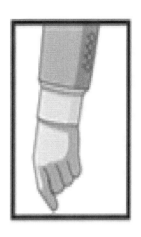 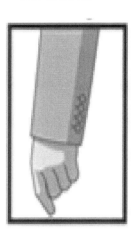

 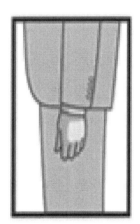 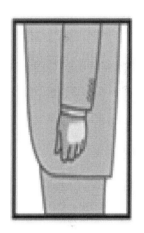

 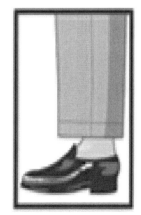 

PERFECT FIT   OFF COLLAR   BUNCHED BACK

Good Fit   **Bad Fit**

There is no limit to the amount of versatility and individuality you can show with a Black or Navy-blue suit *(both of which are a must have in every man's wardrobe)* until you add your shirt and tie. This is one of the few areas of the well groomed man where you can really express yourself. A word of caution though, with these basic suit colors the tie can make or break you; so you may want to get a second opinion before you tie that knot.

The classic navy or black suit combined with a crisp white shirt can be worn with a tie of almost any color or pattern. You can't go wrong

with sheer silks in plain colors. For a safe change, experiment with textures rather than patterns. But if you want to wear a patterned tie, be sure your shirt is plain and vice versa. To mix patterns on both shirt and tie takes keen fashion sense; consult a professional fashion expert before taking this plunge.

As with the suit itself, always go for the best quality when you can afford it. Silk ties are infinitely nicer and hang better than ones made of man-made fibers, while shirts of 100% cotton or a cotton-silk blend look smarter are more comfortable to wear and let your skin breathe. Collars should always be of a classic style, without buttons (wide cut it you plan to wear a big knot), and double or French cuffs that require cufflinks tend to look more stylish than single layer button ups.

It's important to know the best type of collar to get because each type will make your face and upper body look a bit different. There are several different types of collars, but there are a few main ones you should know.

Narrow Spread or Pointed Collar

Medium Spread Collar

Medium Spread Button Down Collar

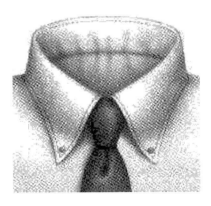

Widespread Collar

Cut-Away Collar

Club Collar or Rounded Collar

WHAT TYPE OF COLLAR IS BEST FOR YOU?

Narrow Face
(you need to broaden your face)
wrong collar: **narrow spread pointed collar** - it makes your face look even thinner
right collar: **widespread collar** - it evens out your face

Round Face
(you need to lengthen your face)
wrong collar: **wide-spread collar-** makes your head look larger
right collar: **pointed or narrow spread collar** - makes your face look thinner

Big Head
(you need to make your head appear smaller)
wrong collar: **pointed or narrow spread collar-** makes your head look even bigger
right collar: **wide-spread or cut-away collar-** makes your head look normal

Small Head
(you need to make your head appear bigger)
wrong collar: **wide-spread collar-** makes your head look even smaller.
right collar: **medium spread**

Long Neck (you need to shorten your neck)
wrong collar: **pointed collar-** accentuates the length of your neck.
right collar: **medium spread or wide spread collar-** gives your face balance.

Short Neck (you need to lengthen your neck)
wrong collar: **short or cutaway collar**
right collar: **narrow pointed collar-** lengthens your neck

The Windsor Knot is a thick, wide and triangular tie knot that projects confidence. It would therefore be your knot of choice for presentations, a job interview, courtroom appearances ...etc.

It is best suited for spread collar shirts and it's actually quite easy to do. While just about everyone can use this knot to tie his tie, it looks especially well on men with longer necks as its wide form shortens the perceived height of the neck a little bit.

❖ *The wide end "W" should extend about 12 inches below the narrow end "N". Cross the wide end "W" over the narrow end "N"*

❖ *Bring the wide end "W" up through the loop between the collar and your tie; then back down.*

❖ *Pull the wide end "W" underneath the narrow end "N" and to the right, back through the loop and to the right again so that the wide end "W" is inside out.*

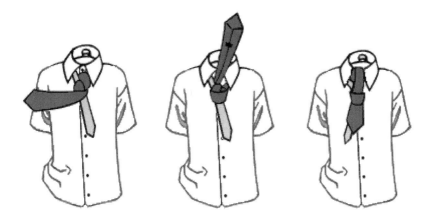

* *Bring the wide end "W" across the front from right to left.*

* *Pull the wide end "W" up through the loop again.*

* *Bring the wide end "W" down through the knot in front.*

* *Using both hands, tighten the knot carefully and draw it up to the collar.*

The Half Windsor Knot, a modest version of the Windsor Knot, is a symmetrical and triangular tie knot that you can use with any dress shirt. It works best with somewhat wider ties made from light to medium fabrics.

The Bow Tie Knot is used to tie a bow tie and is typically worn to give you a formal and elegant appearance. A "black tie occasion" such as a wedding is an event that you would commonly wear a bow tie at, along with a tuxedo.

The bow tie has Croatian roots, dating back to the 17th century. Croatian mercenaries used neckwear, similar to scarves, called the cravat to hold the collars of their shirts together. These were rapidly adopted by the French upper class, which were known as leaders in fashion at the time. Over time, the cravat evolved into the men's neckwear we know today: neckties and bow ties. At the turn of the century, bow ties were an essential part of formal "full-dress" attire. By the 1900s, the bow tie became a staple in men's fashion, often worn by surgeons and academia. While bow ties fell out of everyday fashion after the World War II, it has remained a customary part of formal attire to this day. With today's trendy styles, the bow tie is worn by many as a true fashion statement; even with the more casual dress attire.

Because the bow tie is generally one-size-fits-all, any adjustable bow tie should fit the average (or not so average) man's neck. The neck strap on a bow tie should either have an adjustable slider or a hook and holes with pre-marked measurements. The average neck sizing of a bow tie is 14.5 inches to 17.5 inches. Adjust your bow tie to your neck size and tie it up to see how it feels. It should be snug but not uncomfortably tight (don't asphyxiate yourself). It may take a couple tries to achieve the perfect the fit, but once you figure it out, you'll never have to guess again.

The proper size should never be broader than the widest part of your neck and should **never** extend past the tips of the shirt collar.

❖ Place the bow tie around your neck, situating it so that end "A" is about two inches longer than end "B".

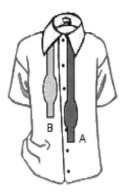

❖ Cross end "A" over end "B". Bring end "A" up and under the loop.

❖ Now double end "B" over itself to form the front base loop of the bow tie.

❖ Loop end "A" over the center of the loop you just formed.

❖ Holding everything in place, double end "A" back on itself and poke it through the loop behind the bow tie.

Adjust the bow tie by tugging at the ends of it and straightening the center knot.

POCKET SQUARES (Handkerchiefs)

Most men would use pocket squares to blow their noses or wipe sweat off their beaded brow. Then, one day some brilliant mind turned it into a piece of fashion.

There are many different ways to fold a pocket square. To perfect the art of folding I suggest perfecting the five folds listed on the following pages, then begin mixing styles and techniques; be creative and think outside the box.

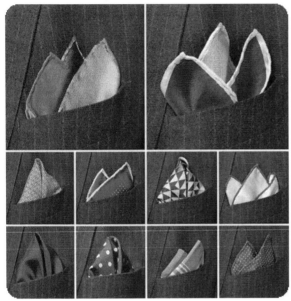

Yes there are common and culturally proper ways to fold your handkerchief, but there is technically no wrong way. So grab your pocket square and suit jacket and just play around until you find a style that fits your personal look.

By creating different folds, you can actually change the look and feel of your outfit. Straight fold is more modern. Corner fold is more traditional. And, puff fold is very, very old school. None the less…

DON'T BE AFRAID TO BE "SQUARE"

If you haven't tried accessorizing your suit, shirt, and tie with a pocket square then here are seven reasons that should be convincing enough to give it a try:

1. A pocket square adds nice color and more live to suit, shirt, and tie.

2. The pocket square is a perfect complement to your neck-tie.

3. A pocket square instantly adds a touch of sophistication and elegance to your ensemble.

4. Using a pocket square allows you to "dress up" or "dress down" an outfit.

5. Best "bang for buck" accessory! - The pocket square earns you lots of style points for little money.

6. Expand your wardrobe - Wearing a pocket square gives the same suit a different look each day.

7. Last but not least, a pocket square allows you to add more personal style to an otherwise uniform looking out-fit.

THE PUFF

1. Lay your pocket square flat with the two top corners horizontal. Pinch the middle of the pocket square and pick it up.

2. As you pick up the pocket square tuck the sides in as in the diagram. Don't worry, it may take a couple of tries to get it just right; but soon you will have it perfect.

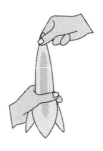

3. With one hand firmly holding the pocket square, use your other hand to gently gather it closed. Now gracefully gather up the bottom of the pocket square.

4. Tuck as needed and place your pocket square in your jacket pocket.

THE PRESIDENTIAL POCKET SQUARE

(Also known as the Flat, Straight, Architect, or TV fold)

1. Lay your pocket square flat with the two top corners horizontal.

2. Fold the left side over the right side.

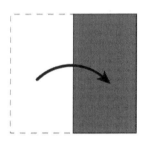

3. Fold the bottom up just short of the top.

4. Tuck as needed and place your pocket square in your jacket pocket.

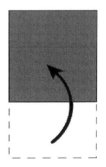

ONE POINT/PYRAMID POCKET SQUARE

(Also known as the one corner)

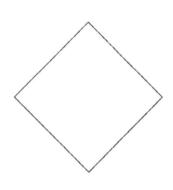

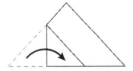

1. Lay your pocket square flat with one corner facing up and one corner facing down.

2. Fold the bottom corner up to meet the

top corner.

3. Fold the left corner to the right.

4. Repeat and fold the right corner in to the left.

5. Tuck as needed and place your pocket square in your jacket pocket.

FOUR POINT POCKET SQUARE

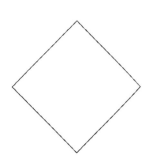

1. Lay your pocket square flat with one corner facing up and one corner facing down.

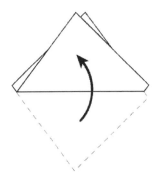

2. Fold the bottom corner up to the top just to the left of the top corner.

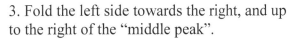

3. Fold the left side towards the right, and up to the right of the "middle peak".

4. Fold the right side towards the left, and up to the left of the "second peak".

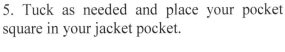

5. Tuck as needed and place your pocket square in your jacket pocket.

DUNAWAY POCKET SQUARE
(combo puff and point)

1. Lay your pocket square flat with the two top corners horizontal. Pinch the middle of the pocket square and pick it up.

2. As you pick up the pocket square tuck the sides in as in the diagram. Don't worry it may take a couple of tries to get it just right, but soon you will have it perfect.

3. With one hand firmly holding the pocket square, use your other hand to gently gather it closed.

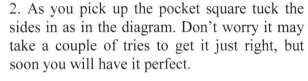

4. Now gracefully roll the top of the pocket square in the direction of the arrow.

5. Carefully lift the bottom points up.

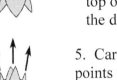

6. Flatten the points.

7. Tuck as needed and place your pocket square in your jacket pocket.

THE BLACK TIE (FORMAL WEAR)

Chances are, if you work in the corporate world, are part of a wedding party or perhaps escorting your "baby girl" to a father daughter ball, you may be called upon to wear a black tie or some type of formal wear from time to time

Whatever the occasion, it should never be viewed as a competition to see how dressy you can get. The whole etiquette of a black tie or formal affair is designed for a man to dress in uniformed attire to complement the woman he is with, be it at the theater, a party or wedding.

Black Tie refers to a **FORMAL EVENING DRESS CODE** that typically requires men to be dressed in tuxedo and women in evening gown. Below is a basic guide on men's black tie attire. It is my goal to make this black tie guide as concise and simple as possible.

The classic black tie dress code consists of a black tuxedo, white dress shirt, black bow tie, and black dress shoes. These items make up the True SWAGGER standard of a black tie ensemble.

The classic black tie tux is solid black in color, is single breasted, has one single button, has a peaked satin-faced lapel, does not have vents at the back, and is made from grosgrain fabric. If you don't want to go with a standard look but still want to stick to the black tie dress code then take note of the following:

ACCEPTABLE TUXEDO COLORS

While black is the classic tuxedo color for black tie functions, a dark midnight blue is an acceptable, and equally suited alternative. Both, black and midnight blue, are acceptable black tie tux colors for evening wear. WHITE DINNER JACKETS worn with black pants are common for *day time* black tie functions. This type of dress code is commonly referred to "warm weather black tie".

TUXEDO CUTS & STYLES

Besides color there are several designs and cuts available when choosing a tuxedo. The most common cut is the single breasted tuxedo. The other choice available is a double breasted jacket. The single breasted style is traditional and more classic. The double breasted cut was introduced in the 1930s. While the single breasted tux is typically worn unbuttoned, the double breasted cut should be worn buttoned.
If you want to keep it traditional then choose the single breasted style, if you want something slightly out of the ordinary then the double breasted jacket would be a suited alternative. Keep in mind that the double breasted cut can be slightly less comfortable when sitting down.

Most classic is the peaked lapel. Slightly less common but equally formal is the shawl lapel. Even though notch lapels are more common nowadays they are considered to be slightly less formal. Typically the lapel has a shiny silk facing that matches the facing on the jacket's buttons.

TUXEDO FABRICS

The classic tuxedo is made from a fabric that has a fine diagonal ribbed texture that is also known as grosgrain. Depending on the quality and price point, tuxedo fabrics range from silk (on the higher end) to a man-made polyester (lowest cost). Most common is fine worsted wool. I suggest you choose a natural fiber such as wool. It is more carefree than silk and much more breathable and comfortable than a synthetic fiber. Choose a wool that is labeled "super 100" or higher. The higher the number; the finer and more exclusive the fabric will be.

Bowties come in many fabrics, colors and patterns- so be careful as you chose the right tie for the occasion. A rule of thumb is the more formal an occasion, the more traditional you need to be. Cufflinks and polished shoes are a must with black tie attire.

RENT VS. BUY

The cost is one of the primary factors to consider when choosing buying vs. renting. If black tie functions are a once in a lifetime event for you then I suggest you go with a rental. Renting a complete black tie outfit will range from $80 to $180. Make sure to that you give yourself enough time for fitting and tai-  loring. Call a rental place ahead of time to see what is available. This can be especially problematic during prom or wedding season.

Buying a tux is a good choice if your body doesn't change too much anymore, and if you plan on attending more than five black tie functions in your lifetime. The classic black tie outfit will not change and just five black tie events can offset the cost of buying your own ensemble.

Other things to consider are design choices, custom tailoring, and quality. Even lower cost tuxedos will be of better quality than a rental. In addition, buying your own tux will allow you to tailor your garment for the perfect fit.

Whether you buy or rent a tuxedo, again you can't go wrong with black or navy-blue. If you have a broader body, remember that a single-breasted will be the most slimming fit. Even some of today's trendy styles can be worn in good taste.

SWAGGER TIP:

THE QUALITY AND FIT ARE
KEY; UNLESS OF COURSE
YOU JUST WANT TO LOOK
LIKE THE WAITER INSTEAD
OF HER DATE.

The classic items that should be found in every man's wardrobe have been around for years and are ageless. ***No matter what generation you fall within***, you really cannot go wrong with a regular cut pair of jeans, sturdy brown boots, a casual jacket, a quality white T-shirt and a V-neck sweater. Every man's wardrobe should consist of these items and variations of them, along with your suit and a selection of shirts and ties, a coat and raincoat.

Of course, it's fine to recommend these basics, but if you walk into any department store, you will be faced with rack of different styles, cuts and variations and colors or denim. Choose to your individual style and taste, but remember you can't go wrong by keeping it simple. The Classic Five Pocket Straight-Leg has been around for over 100 years, so it must be doing something for the Swagger of those who wear them.

GET YOURSELF SOME KHAKIS

Chinos, Combats, Dickeys, Cargo Pants, and Khakis are all pretty much the same thing in that they describe cotton canvas slacks or pants(most often beige), which are a step above jeans but just as relaxed and comfortable to wear. The classic neutral color goes with so much; and the fabric is durable.

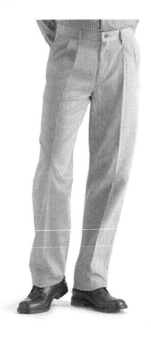

The name Khaki is derived from the Persian word, khak, meaning dust or dirt, and the pants date back to the 19th century army camouflage (the original color was created by dyeing white cotton with tea). There is a style of Khaki to suit everyone's swagger.

SWAGGER TIP: YOU CAN DRESS A
CLASSIC PAIR UP WITH A SHIRT AND
A BLAZER; KEEP IT RELAXED WITH
A SWEATER. KHAKIS AND A CRISP
WHITE SHIRT OF ANY TYPE IS
ALWAYS A CLEAN LOOK.

Polo's are one of the essentials of a *gentleman's* wardrobe. You can easily wear them in a dressy or casual manner. There are hundreds of different types of polo's you can choose from, but always choose quality when it comes to polo.

A mini-history lesson: The polo shirt was first known as a tennis shirt. It was designed by 7-time French Grand Slam tennis pro, Rene Lacoste. He designed it because he needed a more comfortable shirt to play tennis in. He first wore it in the 1926 US Open Championship and in 1927 he added the crocodile emblem. Polo players began to heavily wear the shirt in the 1930's (after Lacoste began to mass produce them); hence the nickname ***"polo shirt"***.   In 1972 Ralph Lauren included the "polo shirt" as a prominent part of his line called Polo, to further boost popularity.

Polo Shirts are iconic. The fact that polo's are a great choice to wear with slacks, khakis, jeans and shorts make them a staple for every man's wardrobe.

Polo shirts are a versatile garment that can be worn for a variety of occasions. Wear polo's to school, to work or wear them for every day SWAGGER. Add a polo shirt to a pair of jeans for a casual outfit that is comfortable to wear. *Going golfing?* Wear it with a pair of shorts and have a comfortably fitting shirt with lots of room to swing a club.

You can even wear a polo shirt with a blazer for a dress up look. If you button up your polo, be sure to wear it with dress slacks, standard fit jeans or pants instead of the baggy styles.

THE WARDROBE

There are 3 main sections in a wardrobe: the core section, defining/signature section, and finishing touches section.

Within your wardrobe, you need to be able to mix and match: so all the sections will include pieces that you will use to create a variety of looks and outfits.

THE CORE

These wardrobe pieces consist of clothing that you absolutely require, are timeless and really capture the essence of any well-dressed man's look. You literally can't live without your core items and they should be a combo of **(your)** personality, practicality and True Swagger.

THE SIGNATURE

This section or layer of your wardrobe should be 80% of you and your style and 20% trend. Sometimes trends end up being a part of your style and that's okay. This section of the wardrobe should also include signature items. Basically these are the clothes that really make your look and capture the essence of your personal style and True Swagger.

THE FINISHING TOUCH

The part of your wardrobe that is all about finishing touches and extra items that you don't need, but really want...

"WHAT'S IN YOUR CLOSET?"

THE CORE

2 pair quality dark denim jeans. Straight, relaxed fit and one pair needed for dress shoes and boots. ***Examples:*** Sevens for All Mankind or Levis (one top quality brand and one good less expensive good quality brand).

1 pair of khakis/chinos/trousersFlat front or pleated depending on your size. Navy or khaki.

1 cardigan in a neutral color Navy, black, or heather gray. ***Example:*** Ralph Lauren, Lacoste.

3 quality white or black t-shirts V or Crew neck (whichever you prefer). ***Examples:*** Slight v-neck Hanes, Calvin Klein

2 Polo's; 1 neutral 1 bright Choose your favorite brand. ***Examples:*** Ralph Lauren or LaCoste, one black one red.

1 button-up any style, color, or brand. It should be one that you really like and it should coordinate with the colors of your other core items. ***Examples:*** 1 Sean John long-sleeve plaid button-up.

(The shoes you pick for your core are totally up to you, they should reflect your style and they are potentially shoes that you could wear everyday with everything.)

1 pair of casual shoes
Examples: navy Vans, black Chucks, white Airforce Ones, brown Sperry boat shoes, neutral colored loafers, casual oxford-type shoe.

1 pair of dressier/less-casual shoes
Examples: oxfords, wing-tips, mid or ankle boots, dressy pair of drivers, Gucci loafer or slip-on.

That is your core and it is timeless… meaning they probably will never go out of style and can easily coordinate with any trend. With these items you can create a variety of looks:

- ➤ *Very casual*: slight V-neck tee, dark denim jeans, and Gucci loafers.

- ➤ *Everyday living*: polo, cardigan, dark denim jeans, Nikes.

- ➤ *Weekend relaxing*: V-neck, cardigan, khakis, boat shoes.

- ➤ *Dressier*: button-up, cardigan, khakis, boots.

Obviously, you don't need to go out and buy everything on this list. Tweak for your specific needs and work dress code, and buy the important stuff first. **Use neutral colors as your Core (black, gray, navy, or tans).** This will not only ensure all your clothes will go together, it also can be a huge time saver.

Look through your drawers and your closet and see what you have to work with, including the old pieces that you haven't worn in a while. Some of those might be surprisingly easy to repurpose while others are destined for the thrift store or the trash heap. *Everyone's core items are going to be a little different. That'll be a part of defining your own **True Swagger and personal style**. Do a realistic assessment and adjust your existing wardrobe as needed.*

THE SIGNATURES

1 pair of colored or your favorite style of jeans
Red, green, blue, or purple *Examples:* LRG, Sean Jean, True Religion, Levis…or any other designer label.

2-4 graphic tees
Choose your favorite type and brand. It should basically fit your overall look. If you have a dressier style then choose tees that would be the "dressed down" version of your look (if that doesn't work then get a t-shirt from your favorite brand *Examples:* Lacoste tee, Coogi, Ed Hardy, Polo).On a Budget: (go to local vintage and thrift stores)

2 jackets (light coat).
A signature jacket and a neutral yet stylish jacket or light coat. Jackets can really set-off the look; it's the icing on a cake… the cake taste good without it, but it taste even better with it. *Examples*: bright

colored aviator jacket, vintage jacket, designer jacket like MCM, or sport coat.

4-6 shirts in the style of your choice
Examples: plaid button-ups, bright colored graphic tees, etc.
Whatever gives you your *True Swagger*.

3 pants/bottoms in the style of your choice
Examples: chocolate colored corduroys, Stone-washed jeans, black jeans, black flat-front trousers, etc.
(Again, whatever gives you your *True Swagger)*

1 pair of Shoes
Choose a pair of shoes that are really stylish to you,
they can be sneakers, dress shoes, or a hybrid of the two. These should be your *"go-get-um"* shoes, the ones that really stand out and make your look. *Examples:* Limited edition Creative Reactions, Marc Jacob sneakers, Kanye West Louis Vuitton shoes, Prada's or a pair of Supras; A pair of Steve Maddens always works.

REMEMBER YOUR SHOES ARE GOING TO EMBELLISH A MAJOR BODY PART, YOUR FEET...WHEN POSSIBLE, ALWAYS PLACE QUALITY AND COMFORT ABOVE COST.

The **SIGNATURE** part of your wardrobe is also where you would include your dressy attire. At some point in their lives, *every* man should own at least one tailored suit in black or navy blue. A tailored suit can cost you anywhere from $200-$2000 depending on where you purchase it. *"My personal favorite is the Steve Harvey line. The cuts, quality, and costs are a favorable mix."*

"ONE SUIT THAT FITS YOU WELL IS FAR BETTER THAN FIVE THAT DON'T"

Accessories
- ❖ Two scarves
- ❖ Two hats (1 fitted, 1 fedora)
- ❖ Two ties
- ❖ A pair of sunglasses.

Just like a jacket can be seen as the frosting on a cake, accessories are the sprinkles and toppings; they complete the cake. Choose accessories that enhance your look. One of these items should be signature, like signature pair of Oliver Peoples glasses or your signature damier LV bookbag, or a signature Fedora.

Examples: scarves, glasses, suspenders/braces, ties, hats, cufflinks. You should own all different types of accessories, but you will have more of one type of accessory depending on your look.

THE FINISHING TOUCHES

These are just the extras; most will probably be trend items.

- **Trendy coat/jacket:** Military or Marching band inspired jacket.

- **Sunglasses:** Wayfarers or aviators.
  Examples: Ray-ban, Tom Ford.
- **Scarves or Ascots**: Plaid, Solids, or designer logo.

- **Jewelry.** Quite frankly, *True Swagger* is not about the "bling bling", although nice at times. Choose a material and color that fits your wardrobe and style. ***Examples:*** one watch and one silver bracelet.

CORE VALUES

Because we live in a world where styles and trends are subject to change at any time, you will never go wrong by adding more basics/core items into wardrobe. And although the items mentioned are all really a matter of personal style and taste, it's a good start for any man looking to create or revamp his wardrobe or enhance his True Swagger.

Be confident in your wardrobe, put thought into it, but don't over analyze it to confusion. Remember one of the most important rules of True SWAGGER:

Keep it simple to keep it stylish.

When in doubt on how to coordinate always resort back to the
True SWAGGER rules of 3;

NEVER MATCH MORE THAN 3 COLORS.

If the information thus far is a bit of a reach or a little too extensive for your personal taste, at least do your best to employ the following basic rules when it comes to your wardrobe and fashion savvy.

Ten Basic Fashion Rules for Men

1. Everything should fit

This might be the most important thing in this list and cannot be stressed highly enough. *Everything* you should buy or even consider in buying must first fit you properly. It is more probable that what you are wearing now is about a size too large. This is understandable because when we were children, our parents usually bought us clothes two sizes bigger than our size so that we may not easily outgrow them. If you believe that you will not gain a considerable amount of weight anytime soon, it is best to buy clothes that fit you well.

"I AM NOT ENDORSING THAT WE SHOULD ALL WEAR SKINNY JEANS. YOU SHOULD ONLY WEAR SKINNY JEANS IF YOU ARE INDEED SKINNY."

2. Your shoes and belt should match

Most of you probably know this but it is still worth noting. Never wear your black belt with your brown shoes and vice versa. Also, avoid wearing your dress belts with your sneakers or your casual belts with your dress shoes.

3. The color of the pants and socks should match

Though there are exceptions to this rule, the most basic thing about this rule is that you shouldn't wear white socks especially when wearing black or charcoal gray dress pants.

WEARING WHITE SOCKS WITH BLACK SHOES IS A STYLE FAUX PAS.

4. Dress for the occasion

A simple rule that is often misinterpreted. I will just point out the essentials of this rule. True Swaggers Law in casual style indicates that the 50's and 60's were the high periods of casual fashion. With today's current trend of "casual or dress-down Friday", people are now throwing away their suits and wearing the t-shirt and jeans in the work setting. If you are a mechanic, plumber or have a dirty job, then you should wear jeans. *In reality, though, casual Fridays should be deemed as Fashionable Fridays.*

5. Do not wear company t-shirts

If you are getting a good amount of money for wearing them then it is totally fine, if not, then consider donating them to the nearest homeless shelter. You should do the same with shirts with sports logos and t-shirts with senseless and ironic messages.
Your t-shirt is not a billboard.

6. Stick to classics; Less is More.

The general rule is that you should wear striking pieces minimally. The rest of the pieces of clothing you are wearing should only be supporting the striking piece. It shouldn't grab or battle for the attention of your most striking showpiece. For instance, a detailed leather jacket works best with plain dark jeans and a simple white shirt.

7. Undershirts

You can ignore this rule and don't wear undershirts, but if you sweat a lot and want your shirts to last longer, then you should wear an undershirt. Crew neck undershirts are still the safest choice to wear, although V-neck undershirts are much applicable if you decide to not wear a tie. If you decide to wear a sheer dress shirt (or see through shirts), don't wear an undershirt unless you want it showing underneath your shirt.

8. The *Wrong* Shoes can ruin your entire outfit.

Women do notice our shoes. Flip flops can only be worn if you intend to go to the beach. Stop wearing tennis and basketball shoes when you go to the mall or at any casual event; they are meant for the gym. For dress leather shoes, look for the traditional round toe as compared to the modern square toe. Lace ups and monk straps look more formal than loafers. Never doubt the presence of a newly polished dress shoe.

9. Wearing designer labels

Being fashionable isn't about wearing the current trend from the hottest designer. ***Don't buy clothes just because of its brand name.*** Not all designer labels produce better merchandise from the average priced retailers. Always check for fit, quality, detail and price before buying. It is always a good idea to buy different items from different labels. Stylish gentlemen usually go to clothing stores but rarely buy. They are known to wait for discounts, sales and even shopping at thrift stores. Fashion can be cheap.

10. Stop being a fashion victim.

Wear what you like and what looks good on you. While you should develop your own personal style, sometimes it is a good thing to copy someone else's style. However, like training wheels, we should remove them once we already know how to balance. Don't become the guy who wears only what his friends wear. Have your own personal style and True Swagger.

There is no two ways about it, fit is the key to the right pants, slacks or jeans. Here are the True Swagger Guidelines to help make sure you make the most of your stride.

- Apart from certain low cut woman's jeans, men's pants are designed to be worn on your waist (not below it). The purpose of this is to hide the slight natural bulge we as men have below the waistline.

- Even with loose fit styles, pants for *real men* are designed to reach the waistline. If your pants don't naturally reach your waistline, the rise is to short; and you send the clear cut message that you need some new ones or you are seeking to draw some extra attention to the area of your body not being covered. Whatever the situation, it's not a good look.

- We could get into the fact of what *saggin* spelled backwards is, or the origin of this style and its Homo-Sexual connotation; but it is my belief that most intelligent men with True Swagger realize that this is not a look desired by most men of good character.

Let's not forget that True Swagger means to present oneself in a positive image. What is positive about wearing your clothing improperly or intentionally showing the world your under garments?

To make the most of your clothes, stick to the basic colors that fit you. While men's fashion sense can vary from one person to the next, new designer clothing lines based upon wealth and entertainment status can lend itself to a wide variety of styles and swagger among our youth, working class, professionals and aspiring entrepreneurs of the fashion world. It may at times be confusing as to what style or trend to follow.

Yet despite the trends, fads and varying styles, *you cannot ignore the fact that people have and will continue to judge you by your appearance.* The harsh reality is that we make decisions about people within the first 3 seconds of meeting them; we then spend the next 90 seconds trying to confirm our first impressions. This means that before you even open your mouth you and your Swagger have been sized up and profiled.

Knowing this, it is *your* responsibility as a man to always dress neatly, professionally, and appropriately. It is also the charge of mature men to set the standard and teach younger men and boys that *Real Men will be:*

The fact is you never know who you are going to meet; at any time you may run into a potential client, a future employer, or for those singles out there, the love of your life. And like it or not, they are going to form their initial impression of you based off of how you look.

And as men, we do well to keep in mind that generally, women make the best style experts; few are the women without strong opinions about what a man should and should not wear.

Trust me, your wife, sister, mother or a stylish female friend *will* tell you the truth about what looks good on you…as well as what doesn't.

**MENSWEAR FOR THE MOST PART IS
ABOUT BEING SMOOTH AND SUBTLE
NOT OSTENTATION AND FLAMBOYANT.
WHATEVER YOU WEAR, WEAR IT WITH
CONFIDENCE WHILE REMEMBERING;**

TRUE SWAGGER

DOES NOT START WITH THE CLOTHES.

CHAPTER 7

HEALTHY

LIVING

THE NEED FOR REGULAR
EXERCISE, GETTING
ENOUGH RECUPERATIVE
SLEEP, KEEPING STRESS
LEVELS UNDER
CONTROL AND EATING
WHOLESOME FOODS
WILL BE OF MORE BENEFIT
TO YOUR
TRUE SWAGGER
THAN ANY PIECE OF
CLOTHING YOU PLACE
ON YOUR PHYSIQUE OR
ANY TOP DOLLAR
COLOGNE YOU MAY
DECIDE TO WEAR.

You may have a closet full of expensive suits, fine linens, and designer jeans; or your shoe game may be "A 1"...but if you are constantly burning the candle at both ends, you will end up looking and feeling as my mother would say *"a hot mess"*.

In order to truly get the most out of your True Swagger, the following information, when applied, will improve your daily swagger, as well as your whole quality of life. If you take care of yourself on the inside and the outside, you could possibly live and look younger longer.

GROOMING ON THE INSIDE

Doing the right things in the bathroom should improve your appearance, sense of well-being and overall swagger enormously, but if you insist on fueling your body with junk food and your daily workout is walking to the car, you will never achieve more than a fraction of your potential to look and feel your best. Your Swagger will be mediocre at best. Not only that, but your energy levels will be much lower than they could be and you will be more likely to suffer from the negative effects of stress.

Do you know the top men's health threats? The list is surprisingly short; including heart disease, cancer and unintentional injury. Thankfully, most men's health threats are largely preventable. Making healthy lifestyle choices, such as eating a healthy diet and including physical activity in your daily routine is a must to maintain True SWAGGER.

It's also important to manage risky behavior, such as drinking too much and engaging in casual sex. Of course, common-sense precautions such as using safety ladders and wearing a seat belt count, too.

What you put in your body and how much you exercise are far more important to the way you appear than the clothing you are wearing or the frequency in which you get a haircut. The good news is that even small changes to your routine will give enormous improvements to your sense of well-being, your general health, how you look....your True Swagger.

EXERCISE

Not exercising is like having your dream car in your garage, which you polish and wax with a passion, but never take on the road; the engine will deteriorate through lack of use.

Research shows that MEN who do not exercise are one and a half more likely to die prematurely than those who do. The benefits of even minimal exercise such as a brisk 20 minute walk three times a week can reduce the risk of heart disease.

The U.S. Department of Health & Human Services Office of Minority Health indicates that due to poor diet and lack of regular exercise, African American Men are 30 to 40% more likely to die from heart disease. If that alone is not incentive enough, Atlanta Georgia based personal fitness trainer, *Mike Bester* says: "Exercise promotes a higher level of blood flow around the body and heart. As fitness levels improve and the demand for blood in the body increases, the body adapts by developing new capillaries, which are directly linked to the quality of your skin and hair. Increased oxygen levels are associated with and improvement in bodily functions on all levels, mentally, physically and sexually.

CREATING A HEALTHIER LIFESTYLE

For many men today, living healthier means not only starting a good, safe exercise routine, but actual weight loss.

Dr. Moshe Lewis, MD and regular contributor of ***healthyblackmen.org*** suggest breaking down your exercise and weight loss goals into smaller, more attainable pieces. Like eating less pork and red meat and more fish and poultry, maybe incorporate a veggie-only day into your life.

We all know that exercise is the starting point for keeping your heart on the go. Staying active obviously helps control weight, assists with reducing blood pressure and improves your mental health. The fact is, anyone is susceptible to a heart attack, although it is widely known that an inactive person is more prone to suffering a heart attack than someone who stays active.

Now to combat this case of slothfulness, all you as an adult male have to aim for are 150 minutes of physical activity each week. Doing something like swimming, brisk walking or climbing stairs that generates aerobic activity is best to help keep the blood flowing at a healthy speed. Of course you can kick it up a few notches or two and do strength training three to five times a week for about 60 minutes max per session. Exercises like squats, lunges, chin ups and dips are also very good for optimal heart health. Regular

exercise is an excellent resolution to have in spite of how difficult it may seem. Proper exercise and good eating habits can help you stave off heart disease, some cancers, and even depression.

Let's face it, no matter how much True Swagger you possess, you're not invincible. If you take better care of your car or favorite electronic gadget than your own health, you are not alone. According to experts at Chicago's Northwestern Memorial Hospital, men's overwhelmingly dismissive attitude towards their health can have dire consequences in the long run.

Move from your man cave to a medical provider to significantly reduce top serious health problems like cancer, depression, heart disease, or even respiratory diseases.

MAN UP...CHECK WITH YOUR PERSONAL PHYSICIAN ABOUT EXERCISE AND YOUR HEALTH TODAY!

1. **Heart Health.** Heart disease comes in many forms, all of which can lead to serious, fatal complications if left undetected. The American Heart Association indicates that more than one in three adult men has some form of cardiovascular disease. *Black men* account for 100,000 more cardiovascular disease mortality cases than white men. Stroke targets an estimated 2.8 million men and high blood pressure is common in younger males. Routine check-ups can help keep that heart beating.

2. **COPD and Other Respiratory Diseases.** Various respiratory diseases usually start with an innocent "smoker's cough." Over time, that cough can lead to life-threatening conditions such as lung cancer, emphysema, or COPD; all of which interfere with normal breathing. According to the *American Lung Association*, each year, more men are diagnosed with and develop lung cancer than in years past. ***Black men are at increased risk for dying from the disease compared to other racial or ethnic groups.*** While exposure to occupational hazards such as asbestos is an increased risk, smoking remains the leading cause of lung cancer.

3. **Alcohol: Friend or Foe?** According to the Centers for Disease Control and Prevention, men face higher rates of alcohol-related deaths and hospitalizations than women do. Men binge drink twice as much and are prone to increased aggression and sexual assault against women. Alcohol consumption increases risk for cancer of the mouth, throat, esophagus, liver, and colon. Alcohol also interferes with testicular function and hormone production, resulting in impotence and infertility. According to the National Bureau of Economic Research, if a problem drinker does not seek help, he is more likely to commit suicide.

4. **Depression and Suicide.** Researchers at The National Institute of Mental Health estimate that at least six million men suffer from depressive disorders including suicidal thoughts annually. If you're depressed, the NIMH recommends these tips:

- Exercise , set realistic goals
- surround yourself with loved ones
- seek professional help

5. **Unintentional Injuries and Accidents.** The Centers for Disease Control and Prevention listed unintentional injury as a leading cause of death for men. This includes drowning, traumatic brain injuries, and fireworks-related mishaps. Motor vehicle death rates for male drivers and passengers ages 15 to 19 were almost twice that of females in recent years. Male workers incur 92 percent of the total reported fatal occupational injuries. Remember: you are not Superman. Be careful.

6. **Liver Disease.** Your liver is the size of a football. Its functions include digesting food, absorbing nutrients, and ridding the body of toxic substances. Liver disease includes conditions such as cirrhosis, viral hepatitis, autoimmune or genetic liver diseases, bile duct or liver cancer, and even alcoholic liver disease.
According to a study posted by the American Cancer Society, alcohol and tobacco use increase your chance of developing liver disease.

7. **Diabetes.** The American Diabetes Association celebrates today's "modern man" as someone who is more aware of his blood sugar health. Men with diabetes face greater risk for sexual impotence and lower testosterone levels, which can lead to increased depression or anxiety. But that's not all: when left untreated, diabetes can lead to nerve and kidney damage, heart disease and stroke, and even vision problems or blindness.
   Your action plan? Healthy eating and exercise.

8. **Influenza and Pneumonia.** Influenza and pneumococcal infection are two leading health risks for some men. Men, who have compromised immune systems due to COPD, diabetes, congestive heart failure, sickle cell anemia, AIDS, or cancer, are more susceptible to these illnesses. The American Lung Association urges older males *(especially African American men and men over the age of 65)* to get vaccinated. Studies show that vaccinations can be up to 70 percent effective in preventing

hospitalizations for both influenza and pneumococcal infection in those over 65.

THE BOTTOM LINE: GET YOUR SHOTS.

9. **Skin Cancer.** According to the Skin Cancer Foundation, men over 50 are at highest risk for developing skin cancer; more than twice the rate as women. Why? ...Because of more sun exposure and *fewer visits to the doctor*. The Centers for Disease Control and Prevention recommend wearing long sleeves and pants, hats with wide brims, sunglasses, and sunscreen when outdoors for either fun or work. Lower your skin cancer risk by avoiding exposure to UV light that comes from tanning beds or sunlamps.

10. **HIV and AIDS.** Men who are infected with HIV may not realize it, as initial symptoms may mimic a cold or flu. However, new infections are on the rise among gay, bisexual and other men who have sex with men. The Centers for Disease Control and Prevention states that *61 percent* of all new HIV infections were attributed to same-sex activity and that 69 percent of new HIV infections were among young males aged 13-29.

THE TRUE SWAGGER
HOME WORKOUT ROUTINE

You don't necessarily have to spend hours in the gym lifting weights or run ten laps around your local track to get a sufficient amount of exercise. It is very possible to achieve and maintain a reasonable level of fitness in and around your own home with very little or no special equipment. The following workout is composed of three parts- *cardio, resistance* and *stretching.* Each part is equally important to obtain a balanced workout. Ideally you should try and do these three times a week.

CARDIO is anything that gets the heart rate going. Go out for a brisk walk, running in place, or ride a bike. Try and do about 20 minutes of continuous exercise, with the first five minutes being a warm up phase and the remaining 15 minutes at an intensity at which you can just maintain a conversation.

RESISTANCE work strengthens and tones your muscles, improving your overall shape and posture. A pair of dumbbells combined with the right amount of repetitions, will not only keep your heart rate going, but can help build enough strength and stamina to take your swagger to new heights.

STRETCHING is the unsung hero of all exercise. Its importance cannot be emphasized enough in helping to avoid injury and increase range of motion safely. It's always best to stretch prior to and at the end of any intense workout.

1 PUSH UPS (20 reps) lie face down on the on the floor with your toes curled under. With your hands shoulder-width apart and upper arms parallel to the floor, push your body up. Keep your body flat and do not lock your arms when you come up from the floor. For a more intense variation, clap your hands at the top of each push-up.

2 SQUATS

Keep your back slightly flexed.

Look straight ahead.

Aim for a 90-degree bend, knees behind your toes.

Keep your weight on your heels.

(20 reps) Stand with your feet facing forward, shoulder-width apart. Bend your knees until your thighs are parallel to the floor, hold, and then push up. Face forward and back straight at all times.

3 CHAIR DIPS (20 reps) Support your body weight with both hands on the edge of a sturdy chair with your heels on the ground and your knees slightly bent. Start with straight arms slowly bending them until your forearms are parallel to the floor, then push up without locking your elbows.

4 LUNGES (20 reps) Stand with your feet together, holding weights in both hands. Take a large step forward with one foot and bend your knees until your back knee is almost touching the floor, then step back up, keeping your knees slightly bent and feet pointing forward. Now repeat the same action with the other foot.

5 OVERHEAD PRESS (20 reps) Holding weights in hands, start with arms bent and hands at shoulder height. Raise your arms together, and then slowly return them to the start position.

6 HAMMER CURLS (20 reps) Standing with your arms by your side and weights in each hand, bend alternate arms toward your shoulder and slowly return them to your side.

7 CRUNCHES (20 reps) Lie on your back (on a towel or mat) with your knees bent and your feet on the floor. Hold your arms out in front of you, or with your elbows pointing outwards, lightly support your head with your fingertips. Raise your head, shoulders, and upper back. Crunch towards your knees, and then lower your body, keeping your head and shoulders of the floor.

8 OBLIQUE CRUNCHES (20 reps) in the same position as above, twist towards alternate knees as you crunch to tighten your sides.

9 STRETCH (2 reps) Sit on the floor with your legs straight out in front of you with your feet flexed. Raise your arms above your head and slowly lower your torso onto your legs, reaching for your feet

"GOOD HEALTH

AND

EXERCISE

GOES HAND IN HAND

WITH HAVING

TRUE SWAGGER"

THE CHALLENGE OF EATING HEALTHY

In the 21st century, one cannot help but be busy. Whether you are a parent, single professional, or student; life is demanding. And too often, we skip the 'the most important meal of the day.' Research shows breakfast improves alertness and concentration; helps prevent overeating during the day. In a real way, eating breakfast can prevent obesity, diabetes, and heart disease.

A diet rich in fresh foods- particularly fruits, vegetables and grains, will benefit your whole body, most noticeably your skin. Healthy skin is dependent on the efficient functioning of the kidneys, intestines and liver. The liver is not only designed to remove waste from the body, but also acts as a filter to harmful chemicals in processed foods and drink, including alcoholic beverages. If your system is sluggish due to a poor diet, the toxins, bacteria and even viruses produced in the body can cause havoc and leave your skin with undesirable spots and blemishes.

As mentioned, few of us manage to really eat a balanced diet rich in *all* the vitamins, minerals needed for optimum health. If you are a Black man, stress is inherently at times a part of life. When coupled with an alternating diet of "fast food" or "take out", it often cause us to give less attention to the vegetables and fruit we need, thus creating a recipe for poor health. If you find yourself concerned about your daily nutrition, taking a daily multivitamin can only benefit you. The following food facts may also help to improve your diet.

- Protein = Power

- Fats and carbohydrates may supply the body with energy, but protein helps regulate the release of that power. Protein maintains cells, assists in growth, transports hormones and vitamins, and preserves lean muscle mass. Muscles and many hormones are, in fact, made up of protein. You need proteins for your immune system. So replenishing your body's source of the nutrient is very important.

Good sources of protein include meat, poultry, fish, eggs, beans, nuts, soy, and low-fat dairy products. When you eat these types of foods, your body breaks down the protein that they contain into amino acids (the building blocks of proteins).

To get these benefits and to prepare the body for the day, the Academy of Nutrition and Dietetics recommends eating carbohydrates for energy and protein for endurance, like:

- Whole grain bagel with cheese

- Cereal with fruit and yogurt

- Whole grain toast with peanut butter and fruit

- Hard-boiled egg sliced into a whole wheat pita

- Scrambled eggs, toast, and fruit

STAY HYDRATED

Being properly hydrated is a quick and easy way to keep your energy high. ***The body needs water.*** For most people, water is the best thing to drink to stay hydrated. Sources of water also include foods, such fruits and vegetables which contain a high percentage of water. Sports drinks with electrolytes may be useful for people doing high intensity, vigorous exercise in very hot weather, though they tend to be high in calories.

You lose water each day when you go to the bathroom, sweat, and even when you breathe. You lose water even faster when the weather is really hot, when you exercise, or if you have a fever. Vomiting and diarrhea can also lead to rapid fluid loss. If you don't replace the water you lose, you can become dehydrated.

Every cell, tissue and organ in your body needs water to function correctly. For example, your body uses water to maintain its temperature, remove waste and lubricate joints. Water is essential for good health.

So keep a fresh and ready source of water by you at all times, and drink at least 1 cup every 2 hours. If you are active during hot summer months, drink more. A person who perspires heavily will need to drink more than someone who doesn't. Certain medical conditions, such as diabetes or heart disease, may also mean you need to drink more to avoid over-taxing the heart or other organs.

Keeping the body hydrated helps the heart more easily pump blood through the blood vessels to the muscles. And, it helps the muscles remove waste so that they can work efficiently.

"If you're well hydrated, your heart doesn't have to work as hard," said John Batson, M.D, a sports medicine physician with Low country Spine & Sport in Hilton Head Island, S.C., and an American Heart Association volunteer.

Dehydration can be a serious condition that can lead to problems ranging from swollen feet or a headache to life-threatening illnesses such as heat stroke. Start missing out on this health essential and you are only setting yourself up for some uncomfortable side effects as dehydration sets in. This can cause everything from headaches and sore eyes to dry skin and chapped lips; all of which can put a crimp in you swagger.

Thirst isn't the best indicator that you need to drink. "If you get thirsty, you're already dehydrated," Batson said.

Dr. Batson advises that the easiest thing to do is pay attention to the color of your urine. Pale and clear means you're well hydrated. If it's dark, drink more fluids. Not sweating during vigorous physical activity can be a red flag that you're dehydrated to the point of developing heat exhaustion. You can stay fully hydrated throughout the day by drinking water and other fluids, as well as eating foods that are hydrating.

WATER IS BEST

Our bodies are made up of about 60% water, and every system depends on water. Water is important for healthy skin, hair, and nails, as well as controlling body temperature, heart rate, and blood pressure. It's healthier to drink water while you're exercising, and then when you're done, eat a healthy snack like orange slices, bananas or a small handful of unsalted nuts.

A word of caution when it comes to fruit juices or sugary drinks, such as soda; they can be hard on your stomach if you're dehydrated. It's also best to avoid drinks containing caffeine, which acts as a diuretic and causes you to lose more fluids.

Drinking water before you exercise or go out into the sun is an important first step; otherwise, you're playing catch-up and your heart is straining.

10 EASY STEPS TOWARD HEALTHY LIVING

1. **Accept that HEALTHY LIVING is an achievable goal**. If you approach exercise and a healthy diet with the concept that small steps will add up to make a big difference over time.

2. **Make a plan to succeed.** Take about a 10-12 *"bad"* food items (e.g. cookies, chips, etc.) off your diet. Plan to start eliminating 1-2 of these items each week. Watch the pounds drop, energy levels increase.

3. **Contact a nutritionist**. Every individual should have a customized nutrition plan tailored to their age, weight, height, metabolism and activity level.

4. **Regular exercise** for at least 30 minutes every day. Enough said.

5. **Set realistic goals**. Rapid results that can't be sustained only results in frustration. The goal should be to achieve a permanent lifestyle change.

6. **Develop a support system**. Surround yourself with others who also seek a healthier lifestyle.

7. **Weigh in regularly**. Don't be afraid of the scale. Every week you should check your weight.

8. **Positive Reinforcement**. Feel good about the changes of success by allowing for small rewards like a massage, purchasing a new CD, etc.

9. **Congratulate Yourself**. Good results can be challenging, so success should be acknowledged for sure.

10. **Really Love Yourself.** Whether you drop five or fifteen pounds, love WHO YOU ARE.

RELAXATION & MASSAGE

Taking the time to wind down is one of the most important things you can do keep yourself in good health. You need to give your mind a proper break from work (or lack of) and any other thing that may plague you with worry on a regular basis. This will keep you happier, less agitated and better able to cope the pressures of everyday life.

One of the best ways to relax is to have an aromatherapy massage, since the soothing physical action eases tension and the essential oils (*page 75*) have a positive effect on emotions and relieve anxiety.

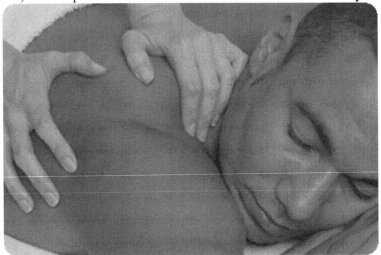

GET RID OF STRESS

Stress can be somewhat tricky, as some stress is necessary while too much is definitely bad. We need stress to get us out of bed in the morning, to challenge ourselves in work or play. However, too much can lead to some real negative effects; sleep may become disrupted, shortness of breath can occur and irritability can set in, along with loss of appetite or eating binges.

Sadly among men, stress has driven someone you know (or someone who knows someone you know) to turn to alcohol or drugs as an escape.

It is so important to learn to control our levels of stress because, besides the negative side effects on our health, it can seriously undermine all efforts toward good grooming and having True Swagger.

THE BIG 6 STRESS
BUSTERS TO LIVE BY

1. CHILL OUT
When get in after a long day, have a shower or bath and get changed into comfortable/casual clothes to put your Swagger into relaxation mode.

2. NO JUNK FOOD
If your idea of relaxing evening is junk food, a few beers and the flat-screen TV…think again, you are only drugging yourself and increasing the toxin levels in your body.

3. TURN IT OFF
Cut your television time in half. You'll be surprised how much extra time you have to yourself...time to learn a new skill or read, which is far more relaxing.

4. GET IN SHAPE
Exercise is a great way of relieving stress and tension.

5. LEARN TO JUST SAY "NO"
If you're at your limit, the measure of true success is being able to pri-oritize and say NO if necessary.

6. TAKE THAT VACATION
BUT DON'T TRY AND DO TOO MUCH. It is far better to see a few sights than to set a hectic schedule that leave you even more exhausted than before you left.

Life is too short to sleep all the time.

But life is also too short not to sleep a large part of the time.

The fact is we need sleep, between 7–8 hours a day. But most of us aren't getting it. According to studies from the Centers for Disease Control and Prevention, sleep deprivation is epidemic.

If you don't get enough sleep, it will soon show. The blood in your body is redirected away from your skin to your over exhausted organs. Leaving you face with dark circles beginning to form under your eyes.

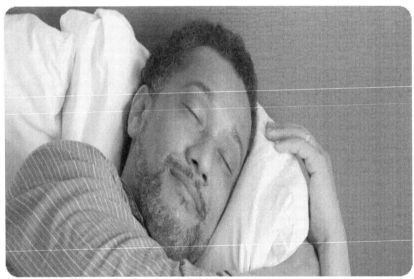

Lack of sleep negatively affects your memory recall and powers of concentration, so you will perform less efficiently. If you find it difficult to have a restful sleep, try going to bed at a regular time to get into a better sleep routine. Avoid caffeine during the late afternoon (even tea and chocolate contain caffeine). Chamomile tea is a great sleep enhancer. Alcohol can make sleep erratic, although it may make you fall asleep faster, that shot of cognac or whiskey will not make your sleep more restful. Regular exercise should help your sleep as it stops the buildup of stress hormones that interfere with sleeping.

CHAPTER 8

GROOMING FOR THE MIND

Made within a few seconds, first impressions are powerful and should not be taken lightly. We often observe a person before we speak with them, and being human we look to make sense of what our eyes are showing us. Using our personal experiences, we categorize individuals; we pick-up on a key feature that has meaning to us and then associate that person with it. If what you are wearing is doing all the talking for you, make sure it is sending the message you want.

Properly clothing yourself takes time; shirts need to be ironed, shoes shined, and jackets brushed. Perhaps the greatest lesson this teaches is to respect the effort put forth by our fellow human beings. When you meet another well-dressed man, why not develop the "mind set" to give him an extra measure of respect because of his Swagger. Mutual respect between all men is garnered when they recognize the efforts each has put forth. To be a true gentleman, you need to be self-aware, mature, and courteous. Though chivalry isn't dead, you can make an effort to bring more respect and care into the world.

With clothing covering 90% of your body, it can't be stressed enough as to how important a role it plays in how you are perceived by others. Want faster & better service in a restaurant? Look like you have money and wear a navy blazer. Want to increase your chances for an A on a college presentation? Wear a sports jacket and pair of slacks. Want instant credibility in a business environment? Wear a suit when making the pitch or meeting with management.

Truly over 75 percent of the success, happiness ….and yes, True Swagger you will develop in life is going to be determined by the overall quality of the relationships you develop in your personal and perhaps business activities. The more people who you know and who know you in a *positive* way, the more appreciated and respected your Swagger will be.

Whether in business or life, your Swagger can be the fine line between success and failure; the difference is in your "mind set" and the choices that follow.

Our society is a case in point for the need to embrace the understandable and, ultimately, achievable principles of being a gentleman with True Swagger.

BEING MALE DOES NOT GUARANTEE A BOY WILL GROW UP TO BE A GENTLEMAN AND THE CURRENT SELF-ABSORBED CULTURE IS NOT LIKELY TO MODEL OR PROMOTE THE QUALITIES OF A GENTLEMAN. IT IS A PROCESS FOR A BOY TO BECOME A MAN AND DEVELOP INTO A GENTLEMAN.

Parents invest a great deal of time and resources to develop their son's academic, athletic, or artistic talent, with little or no thought as to what is required for him to mature into a gentleman.

A gentleman understands that his appearance, behavior, and way of communicating provide others with valuable insight into his character. He knows that he did not acquire his true strength at the gym. Rather, he demonstrates true strength through his strong character and integrity. Therefore, the art of being a gentleman is relevant for today, and it is accessible to every man; young and old.

"BEING A GENTLEMAN NEVER GOES OUT OF STYLE"

THE TRAITS OF A GENTLEMAN

1. *A gentleman is generous with his time, wisdom, and resources.* He willingly serves others and extends a hand to those in need.

2. *A gentleman possesses a positive outlook on life.* His humor and consistent encouragement attract others to him.

3. *A gentleman is a lifelong learner.* He maintains a teachable posture and embraces change for the better.

4. *A gentleman models civility in how he treats others.* He demonstrates respect, restraint, and personal responsibility in all his interactions. He is honorable, and values and respects others.

5. *A gentleman is well-mannered and knows what is appropriate.* He is able to navigate various social and professional settings with ease and proficiency. He embraces all people; those from other cultures, as well as individuals from various social and economic backgrounds.

6. *A gentleman possesses a strong work ethic.* He takes pride in his labor and strives to give his very best. He is trustworthy, loyal, and people speak well of him.

7. *A gentleman is confident.* His posture and body language communicate a strong personal presence.

8. *A gentleman is well-dressed.* He knows how to select clothing that is appropriate for any occasion and that will assist him in accomplishing his goals. He is well-groomed and practices good hygiene. He understands that his personal appearance; the way he chooses to dress, groom, and carry himself; opens doors to new opportunities.

9. *A gentleman is well-spoken and a generous listener.* He knows how to effectively connect with others and communicate his message.

10. *A gentleman is known for his integrity.* He is a man of his word and follows through with his commitments, whatever the cost. His actions reflect who he has chosen to be and are not based upon the opinions of others.

"BEING MALE IS A MATTER OF BIRTH, BEING A MAN IS A MATTER OF AGE, BUT BEING A GENTLEMAN IS A MATTER OF CHOICE." *~UNKNOWN*

Final Note

Men aren't just born with Swagger, there's a lot more that goes into the equation. I've found those men who are highly successful have a lot more in common than we may think. If you're seeking success and True Swagger, knowing these things may come in handy:

1. Fail. No matter how hard you work, failure can and will happen. The most successful people understand the reality of failure, and its importance in finding success. Rather than running and hiding when you fail, display some true swagger, embrace it. Learn from this mistake and you won't fail in the same way again.

2. Set goals. Those who are successful set daily achievable goals. Find your True Swagger by solidifying smart, measurable, attainable, realistic, timely goals. Stop juggling a mental to-do list of just long-term goals and establish small daily goals to achieve your vision, your style... your swagger.

3. Don't rely on Chance. Many relate your success to being in the right place at the right time. While this is an element of success, there's also the crucial involvement of blood, sweat, and tears. Don't hold yourself back by waiting for the perfect timing or idea. Some of the most successful people got there by hitting the ground running, even if timing wasn't perfect.

4. Track progress. Success comes from regularly monitoring behaviors, strategies, and tactics. How can you make adjustments if you don't know how you're doing? Hold yourself accountable by checking your progress as often as possible.

5. Act. Successful people don't always know the right answer, but the keep moving anyway. Don't let obstacles stall you when you're searching for the right solution. Taking action will lead to answers.

6. Connect the dots. Those who are successful have the ability to see the greater picture. They identify and connect the tiny details to get there. Look at things in a "past, present, and future" context to receive favorable results.

7. Display realistic optimism. Those who succeed truly believe in their abilities. This is what true swagger is all about. Assess your abilities to gain a clear understanding of what you are able to accomplish.

8. Continued improvement. Successful people habitually thrive on self-improvement, whether it's in terms of learning from mistakes or simply using their weaknesses as opportunities. Channel this habit by continually searching for ways to be better.

9. Commit. To be successful in both life and work, it takes commitment that doesn't wane. It takes believing that you can create movement in your life and business, even when the waters are still. Throw yourself into your tasks and go the extra mile every single day. Make no exceptions.

10. Persevere. True Swagger requires that you never give up. Might you experience failures? Yes. But as times get hard, your stamina to move forward will not wane. Develop a willingness to work through the challenges you encounter along the way.

11. Display humility. The most successful individuals lack an ego. It's their fault when they fail. Hold yourself accountable for every aspect of your life by focusing on remaining focused and humble.

12. Make connections. Successful people often attribute their achievements to the help of others. You can't and won't be able to do this alone. Invest in generating mutually beneficial relationships.

When it come to the character of a man, the old adage hold true... *"You shouldn't judge a book by its cover",* but in our fast paced society a book's cover can be just as important as its content. Of course appearances are not everything; you have to perform well to succeed, no matter how you measure success.

In this competitive world it pays to understand the importance of your dress and grooming. Investing the proper resources into your personal presentation will multiply your ability to succeed, be a Gentleman, and have ...

...

TRUE SWAGGER.